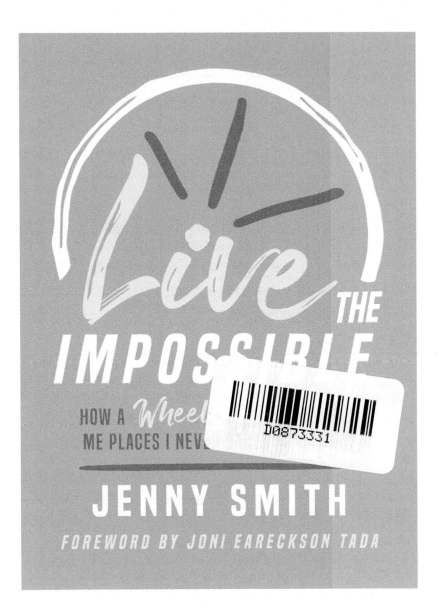

Live the Impossible

HOW A *Wheel...* ME PLACES I NEV...

JENNY SMITH

FOREWORD BY JONI EARECKSON TADA

SIGNIFICANT

-PUBLICATIONS-

Live the Impossible:

How a Wheelchair has Taken Me Places I Never Dared to Imagine

by Jenny Smith

Published by Significant Publications

Paperback: 978-1-7370867-0-3

Digital Online: 978-1-7370867-1-0

For more information, email Jenny@JennySmithRollsOn.com.

First paperback edition May 2021.

Book design by Jenneth Dyck

Editing by Beth Jusino and Kathy Burge

Formatted for Publication by Ben Wolf - www.benwolf.com/editing-services/

This book may be purchased in bulk for proper promotional, educational, or business use. Please email Jenny Smith at Jenny@JennySmithRollsOn.com for more information.

The events and conversations in this book have been set down to the best of the author's ability, although some names have been changed to protect the privacy of individuals.

To my mom and dad, and the "World's Coolest Grandma," thank you for allowing me to live the impossible.

FOREWORD

Having lived with quadriplegia for over fifty years, I am comfortable with my life being on display. Whether a child studies my wheelchair, or a waiter eyes me as I use a bent spoon to eat my meal, I'm aware people are watching.

Hopefully, they are learning something. Something about attitude and perseverance. If so, that's good. At the end of the day, it helps me to look over my shoulder and think, *My wheelchair's worth it.*

It's why I am drawn to the story of Jenny Smith. She is fully aware that her quadriplegia is on display and is not about to be careless with the hand she's been dealt. This woman has sense and sensibility, given the way she creatively stewards the influence God has given her. I admire that.

But it is not the only reason I'm attracted to her.

The Bible tells a story about an impossible situation in which even Jesus's disciples woefully throw up their hands and complain, "This can't be done." The Lord steps in and as much as says, "Your faith is too small; for with God, *all* things are possible."

Jenny must have large faith because she makes the impossible look easy. Just watch her chop up meat in a frypan, and you'll see what I mean. Can't break up the hamburger? Try a spatula. If that doesn't work, use the rocker knife. And if it slips from your paralyzed hands? Push forward with a grin.

Here is a quadriplegic who defines how to live the impossible. She's got a great attitude, and an even greater propensity to persevere.

Jenny's life is all about serving others. Through her tireless efforts and whirlwind schedule, she is helping thousands of people learn how to overcome adversity with a smile.

Whether it's through her wise and wonderful blog posts, her one-on-one mentoring, her athletic prowess, or her helping paraplegic women pick out the perfect pair of Pappagallos, Jenny doesn't stop. This wheelchair-user has forged a carpe diem lifestyle, constantly squeezing opportunities out of every moment.

One more thing. Please don't think Jenny is a plaster-saint who never tastes the setbacks common to quads. I know how demoralizing the challenges of living with high-level quadriplegia can be, and Jenny has felt the sting of disappointments and the regret of lost dreams. Perhaps it's why her optimism is tempered with a gutsy realism.

All of it helps her live Godward and outward . . . *never* inward.

I *like* Jenny Smith. If we lived close and could park our wheelchairs together, I know we'd be good friends. I am drawn to her sunlit personality and her streetwise savvy when it comes to dealing with a disability on a daily basis.

The woman whose story you hold in your hands may be lacking fingers that work and feet that walk, but she makes up for it in heart. From the first chapter to the last, your spirit will soar as you learn about a sister whose soul is settled, whose peace is profound, and whose zest for life is *invigorating*.

So pour your favorite cup of coffee, get comfortable, flip the page and get to know your new friend, Jenny Smith.

Like me, you will think, *If this young woman can overcome her limitations with grace and dignity, then surely, I can learn to smile too . . . not despite my difficulties but because of them.*

It's the way you live the impossible.

Joni Eareckson Tada
Joni and Friends International Disability Center

CHAPTER ONE

My phone chimed with an incoming text message one night while I was washing off my makeup. It was Sydney, a nineteen-year-old woman with a new spinal cord injury. I'd met her recently in a restaurant parking lot, and we discovered we had mutual friends when I noticed she was using one of my old wheelchairs. I gave Sydney my number and told her to text if she had any questions or to call if she wanted to talk. She had reached out several times since then, asking common questions about life with a spinal cord injury. I wondered what she was thinking about tonight.

I read her text message:

Hey, Jenny. The one-year anniversary of my injury is tomorrow, and I know you've been through quite a few of these days. This is probably a dumb question, but do you have anything you do to get you through the day or anything that's helped you?

I pondered her question as I brushed my teeth, changed into my pajama top, and transferred into bed using a sliding board—activities that at one point had been impossible for me to do by myself.

I reflected on the first few years after my injury. Those anniversaries were the hardest as I looked back and craved the life I used to live. A life full of independence, physical ability, and freedom in its many forms.

For the first several years after my accident, my losses were greater than my accomplishments. I depended on others for my every physical need. I had lost my identity as an athlete and floundered as I tried to figure out who I was as a person with a disability. I hated the changes I saw in my body. It took years to accept I was never going to walk again. It took even longer before I could accept myself without needing to prove my worth to the people around me. Life was hard. Well, let me be honest: life is still hard.

The year before my spinal cord injury, when I was fifteen years old, I attended summer camp in North Carolina. One evening, the leaders instructed us to find a quiet place and simply be still and listen. I chose to go outside. Under the clear sky, I lay down and soaked in my surroundings. The bright stars shining in the darkness. The majesty of the mountains. The dense trees of the forest. Insects making a cacophony of sounds. God was simply *there*. The following words came to me, and I wrote them in my journal.

The path before me is long and narrow
It's an uphill battle that will be a struggle

I wanted to know the rest of the story, but no other words came to me, even after months of reflection. And I'm glad. I'm glad God didn't show me all that was to come. It would have paralyzed me—no pun intended.

The path set before me at age sixteen was full of potholes, cobblestones, and gravel. It continues to be bumpy, uncomfortable, and tiresome. But it's also been beautiful, rewarding, and adventurous.

I wondered where Sydney was on this journey. Only one year had passed since her injury, and I assumed she was asking the same questions I had: Why me? What can God ever accomplish with a broken body? Why wasn't I headlined on the nightly news as the girl who marched across the stage to receive her high school diploma because of her ceaseless determination? *Why?*

A future full of possibilities wasn't yet on my horizon. I didn't dream of traveling to Mexico. Certainly not to Afghanistan. I didn't think I'd ever compete as an athlete again. I wouldn't play tennis or rugby, or row in regattas. Model during New York Fashion Week in *this* body? Never. And I believed it would be impossible to live on my own as a quadriplegic.

All of this was a future I never dared to imagine.

My story isn't one of miraculous healing—at least not of physical healing. I didn't overcome the statistical odds of regaining the use of my body after a spinal cord injury. I still use a wheelchair after more than thirty years.

And *that*, my friends, is the miracle.

I wondered if Sydney would eventually see the possibilities for her life. Would she get out of her comfort zone, even when it's terrifying? Would her faith be stretched as mine had? I could only hope that Sydney would have the courage to live the impossible.

CHAPTER TWO

On that hot summer evening of July 10, 1989, my best friend Barbara and I were in the swimming pool in her backyard. My sun-kissed blonde hair sat in a ponytail high on the crown of my head as we lounged on the steps of the pool. Cicadas buzzed and fireflies twinkled in the backyard of her home in the East End of Louisville. A pink and lavender bikini hugged my lean yet muscular sixteen-year-old body.

Barbara's family had taken me in while my parents and younger brother enjoyed the white beaches of Destin, Florida. I'd passed up a rare family vacation to not miss a day of cheerleading practice before our big competition the following week. As one of the stronger members of the squad, I thought it was important for us to practice as a team throughout the next week.

With the sun beginning to set, Barbara and I chatted about nothing in particular as teenage girls do. She told me about a woman at her church who recently had a brain stem stroke. She was paralyzed from the neck down.

"What do you think it would feel like to be paralyzed?" Barbara asked.

"I don't know. I wonder if it hurts?" I swirled my legs back and forth through the warm water. "I've heard you can't feel anything."

"Would you know how to move your legs but just couldn't make them move?"

After a few moments of contemplation, I stepped out of the pool and wrapped a towel around myself. "I can't imagine what that would be like," I said.

I walked to the house, entered the basement door, and bounded up the stairs two at a time to take a shower before going to bed.

The next morning, I drove to cheerleading practice in my mom's blue Toyota Corolla. I'd had my driver's license for only five months, but I loved the freedom driving had given me. I no longer depended on my mom for rides, and that gave me such a sense of being "grown up."

Barbara was taking a college placement test that morning and would come to practice later. She was a year older than me and going into her senior year of high school. We had been friends both in and out of the gym ever since we met in gymnastics after I moved to Kentucky from the suburbs of Chicago when I was almost eleven years old.

Cheerleading practice was typically in the school's small gym, but the competition would take place outdoors. The team decided to practice in the park across from the school. I grudgingly crossed the street in the muggy summer heat to the grassy area inside the paved loop of Seneca Park where people were taking their morning jogs. We rehearsed our five-minute routine multiple times with its combination of tumbling, cheering, and a choreographed dance program.

Having grown up in competitive gymnastics, my tumbling and jumping skills were what drew me to cheerleading. In my dreams, I still feel my muscles tightening, toes pointing, and the explosive, controlled power needed to propel my body through the air.

After practicing for more than a half hour, while everyone else took a brief break, I continued tumbling.

I began doing a round-off back handspring layout, finishing with the backflip rotating high in the air with my body extended straight. It was a move I had perfected in elementary school.

I hadn't noticed the grass was wet with the morning's dew. While taking off for the layout, I saw the trees and sky beginning to rotate as my legs launched me off the grass, but my body didn't float through the air as it normally did, and the ground appeared too quickly. I didn't have enough height or rotation to make it back around to my feet.

In a fraction of a second, my forehead hit the ground, and my body crumpled. I was on my stomach, face-first in the grass. I heard a popping sound upon impact.

I was conscious, but it took a moment to realize what had just happened. I couldn't move or feel any part of my body. My arms and legs were lifelessly sprawled in the grass.

I heard my friends' feet crushing the grass as they ran to me.

"Jenny, are you okay?"

"I've broken my neck. Don't move me."

I was stating—what seemed to me—an obvious fact. I couldn't recall where or when I learned that you shouldn't move someone who was paralyzed, but I knew that's what had happened.

As I lay on my stomach with my face in the grass, my main worry wasn't that I couldn't move. *What if bugs crawl toward me? I won't be able to get away from them!*

Other than the fear of those imagined bugs, I felt no panic. No fear.

I heard Barbara's mom kneel at my right side. Mary Ann had previously worked as a medical technologist in an emergency room. Whether it was her training or, as she believes, a prompting from God, she had the instinct to ask an important question.

"Jenny, can you feel this?" she asked while touching somewhere on my body. "How about here?"

"No," I told her. "Mary Ann, I think we need to pray."

Having grown up in church and participated in youth group and Bible studies, turning to God in this critical situation was my first response.

Sitting next to me in the grass, Mary Ann prayed out loud. I don't remember what she said, but I knew this was going to be one of the most important prayers of my life. At some level deep in my soul, I understood that what just happened was life-changing. I was going to need to rely on God in ways I never had.

Mary Ann told me an ambulance was on its way. Controlling the situation the only way I could, I realized that if I was going to a hospital, then I needed identification and insurance. "The insurance card is at my house on a shelf near the kitchen."

"I don't think we need to worry about that right now, Jenny."

As we waited for an ambulance to arrive, someone brought a bag of ice from the school cafeteria and placed it on the back of my neck. But I couldn't feel the ice. Other than the grass tickling my face and the warm sun beating down on my head, I felt nothing. No tingling or burning. My neck didn't throb with pain. It was as if my body didn't exist below my head.

I heard the ambulance pull onto the thick grass and saw the paramedic's shoes approaching me, step by step.

He leaned down at my left side. "We're going to take good care of you, Jenny. Okay?"

"Okay."

"I see you have a necklace around your neck. I'm going to have to cut that off."

Dread rushed over me. The simple gold cross didn't hold much monetary value, but I wore it to remind me of the foundation of Christian faith on which I lived. The necklace held memories of gymnastics, youth group, summer camp, and playing the piano.

"Please don't cut it," I begged. I was more concerned about my necklace than my current physical condition.

The paramedic must have heard the panic in my voice.

"Let me see what I can do." He scooted the necklace around and unclasped it without cutting it.

I let out a sigh of relief.

"All right. Now we're going to put a neck brace on you and get you onto the stretcher."

I felt the hard foam and plastic rest against my chin and the back of my skull as he placed the brace on my neck. As they rolled my body onto my back, my eyes no longer focused on the green grass, but the bright blue sky.

I'd later learn that as they cautiously turned my body onto a stretcher and loaded me in the ambulance, Barbara had arrived and was leaning against a tree, crying. Mary Ann had to make the heart-wrenching choice between comforting her daughter or accompanying me to the hospital. She climbed into the ambulance.

The ride to the hospital was not what I expected. *Isn't an ambulance supposed to go fast and have sirens?*

Instead, it was quiet and felt like we were inching ever so slowly through the streets. Only now do I understand that the EMS driver was taking every precaution to keep my neck and spinal cord stabilized.

"Can you breathe okay, Jenny?" the paramedic repeatedly asked.

After hearing this question several times, I started to get paranoid. *Can I breathe okay?* I took a deep breath. Yes, I could breathe. I didn't know that a spinal cord injury similar to mine could have prevented me from breathing without assistance.

In an attempt to overcome the fear of the unknown that was beginning to churn deep within me, I focused my thoughts on my plans for the rest of the day.

"Mary Ann, will you call the guys and tell them I may not be at band practice?"

When we arrived at the nearby hospital, the paramedics pulled the stretcher out of the ambulance. With my neck in the brace, I could see only what was directly above me, mostly the tops of people's heads. I watched the ceiling tiles pass by above me as I was pushed into the ER. I heard the emergency room staff tell me they were going to cut off my clothes.

First my necklace. Now my clothes?

I had saved money and recently bought the new blue spandex shorts.

"I just got them. Do you have to cut them?" I asked.

I still felt nothing below my neck, but the sound of scissors cutting fabric confirmed that they did, indeed, need to cut off my clothing.

I don't remember much after that, except being put back into another ambulance. As we drove across town, my head ached with a dull pain. I felt the ambulance descend a steep entrance to Kosair Children's Hospital in downtown Louisville.

My grandma had arrived in Louisville a week earlier for a visit, and she was still at our house with plans to drive to Cincinnati that day. A pastor from my church called her to ask her to come to the hospital immediately. After arriving at the hospital and hearing the critical nature of my injury, Grandma called my parents in Florida.

"Jenny's been in an accident," Grandma told my mom.

"How bad is the car?"

Since I was a relatively new driver, that seemed like the most reasonable explanation for an accident. After thirteen years of gymnastics, no one expected me to be severely injured while tumbling.

In a daze, my mom purchased an airline ticket, packed her suitcase, and caught a flight to Louisville all within a few hours. Only after seeing my grandma and three of the moms from school waiting for her at the gate did Mom realize the seriousness of my injury.

Mary Ann walked up, hugged her, and simply said, "It's bad."

In the meantime, my dad, along with my brother and a friend, drove twelve hours from Destin to Louisville in a heavy rainstorm. Every year on the anniversary of my injury, my brother lovingly—teasingly—reminds me how I ruined his Florida vacation.

~

The ten days I spent in intensive care are hazy. My mom spent each night with me. I don't recall in what order things happened, but I have vivid memories. Some I still laugh about, recognizing that even in the ICU, I was a typical teenager. Other memories break my heart knowing that no sixteen-year-old should ever go through an experience like mine.

In the dark room, flat on my back in bed, there was no day or night. The medication the nurses gave me had me in and out of consciousness.

With my parents at my bedside, I remember the neurosurgeon coming into the room and saying matter-of-factly, "You have damaged your spinal cord at the sixth and seventh vertebrae. You will never walk again."

With the pretentious attitude of a teenager, I replied, "I know. I told *you* that."

After all, I *had* told my friends I'd hurt my spinal cord.

But it would take months to understand the full impact of an injury. A spinal cord injury is so much more than just not walking. An injury in the cervical, or neck, region at the sixth and seventh vertebrae is called a C6-7 spinal cord injury. The injury paralyzes its victim from the chest down and affects the hands, wrists, and arms. When I was in intensive care, I could shrug my shoulders and slightly move my wrists to the beat of the heart monitor. As the swelling decreased in my spinal cord, it was possible I'd regain more use of my arms, but only time would tell. The doctor told me there was only a one percent chance of ever walking again—a statistic that was accurate at that time.

Within the first few days, I remember the room feeling crowded with a doctor, several nurses, and my mom. I heard the whirring of a drill. I felt pressure, but no pain, while the doctor drilled long metal rods into my skull near my ears for traction. The doctor had administered a shot to prevent the pain, but my brain was so muddled I couldn't understand why it didn't hurt. The doctor hoped the weight pulling my skull away from my body would realign my dislocated vertebrae and relieve the pressure, swelling, and bruising on my spinal cord. The saying "I broke my neck" is only an expression in my case. I didn't break the bones in my neck. It was the dislocation of the two vertebrae that caused my paralysis.

"We've drilled in the wrong place. We're going to have to redo it," someone said.

I heard my typically timid mom insist, "She will *not* be awake if you have to do this again."

A doctor or nurse must have pushed some medication into the IV because I drifted off immediately.

Another day, I had a vivid dream of seeing my youth pastor from middle school. When I woke up, I excitedly told my mom, "I had a dream that I got to see Danny!"

"Danny was here to see you, but you couldn't stay awake."

In my drug-induced state, I hadn't dreamed of his visit; I just wasn't conscious enough to actually talk with him. Danny and his wife had shown me how to make my faith my own. When I was thirteen, I decided to be baptized, representing my belief that Jesus was born the Son of God, died to forgive my sins, and was raised from the dead. Going to church was not just a ritual I did on Sundays to please my parents or be with friends. I learned to trust God by seeking His direction for my life by reading my Bible and writing prayers in journals each night. I was crushed to have missed the chance to see Danny.

I remember the panic and fear of a nightmare in which a demonic, pterodactyl-like creature was backing me into a corner. Either in reality or in the dream, I was gasping for air and yelling for help, but no one came to my rescue. I felt alone, trapped, and defenseless. No one was coming to my rescue. I still wonder if it was a dream or a spiritual attack.

I remember laughing as some friends—Kevin, Scott, and David—enthusiastically filled exam gloves with water and had "water glove" fights. In my private room in the intensive care unit, flat on my back in traction, the cold water sprayed me as I lay watching and laughing at their misadventures. These same friends earnestly supported me when the sides of my long hair were shaved to insert the traction rods. I had been devastated, but when they came to my room, the guys showed me they had shaved the sides of their heads too. I smiled and rolled my eyes in response to another one of their crazy escapades. Their diversions filled a void of isolation and sadness that I couldn't yet express.

Six days after my injury, I remember being prepped for the spinal fusion surgery that would stabilize my vertebrae. I felt the pressure of the nasogastric tube forced up my nose. Warm, thick blood flowed down my throat. The world went dark as the anesthesia knocked me out. Bone from my hip and small screws and wire would hold the vertebrae together so they could heal in the proper position.

I remember being asked what I wanted to eat for the first time after surgery. I blurted out the first thing that came to mind, "Belgian waffles." Oh, the first bite of the crispy, soft waffle, drenched in sweet maple syrup was delightful.

I remember Barbara coming in and sitting beside me

silently while I listened to "Strong Medicine," a song by Bryan Duncan. A tear or two trickled down the side of my face as I resonated with the lyrics, wondering if there was any hope. I wasn't able to describe my feelings. And to be honest, I'm not sure I even had any. Although I say I felt nothing, the fact is those tears represented *something*, even if I couldn't put a name to it.

As she sat beside me, Barbara saw the traction rods sticking out of my head. She was thinking, *This cannot be real.* She wanted to ask me the very questions we had talked about the night before my injury while we sat on the steps in the pool, but she didn't want to make me uncomfortable. She didn't feel it was the right time to talk about it. It took twenty-seven years for us to find the right time.

While I was lying in the darkened ICU room, I remember my dad telling me that a large convention of churches was gathered in Louisville and thousands of people at the event were praying for me. Maybe the prayers of thousands of people would be enough for God to heal me. It certainly didn't seem like He'd heard any of my prayers.

To boost my spirits, I repeated a well-loved verse from the Bible. "Those who hope in the Lord will renew their strength. They will soar on wings like eagles; they will run and not grow weary, they will walk and not be faint" (Is. 40:31 NIV). This verse that I knew by heart was a clear promise that God would allow me to run and walk again. Surely, He would follow through on His promises.

Despite the traction to relieve the pressure on my spinal cord and the spinal fusion to stabilize my neck, these weren't enough to prevent paralysis. These days, with medication to relieve the swelling and surgery performed within the first twenty-four to seventy-two hours after injury, more people with injuries like mine are regaining some feeling or function below their level of injury. But at the time of my injury, neither of these were standard practice.

I try not to wonder "What if . . . ?"

Eleven days after my accident, I was finally upgraded from the ICU to a regular hospital room. I was allowed to get out of bed and sit in a recliner for the first time. It was odd to watch—but not feel—the nurse move my legs over the edge of the bed until my feet rested on the sterile white floor. I felt completely vulnerable as the nurse wrapped her arms around my body, picked me up, and pivoted me in one swift motion into the recliner.

I felt woozy, and my vision started fading. "I think I'm going to pass out."

I didn't know that my injury prevented my body from regulating my blood pressure, body temperature, heart rate, and even digestion.

The nurse reclined the back of the chair and pulled my hair over the headrest, displaying the sides of my head that had been shaved. The neck brace I'd received after surgery sat uncomfortably beneath my chin, preventing me from moving my head from side to side or up and down. But I was able to see my entire room for the first time, decorated with balloons, cards, and stuffed animals from friends and family. After a while, the nurse put the back of the recliner more upright, and I tolerated it this time without feeling dizzy.

Friends and family normally filled my room. During a lull in the activity, while my room was uncommonly empty, a woman walked in. She looked familiar, although I couldn't place her.

"Jenny, I'm Melissa Forsythe from WHAS11 TV. May I interview you?"

My accident happened before Congress passed strict privacy laws commonly referred to as HIPAA. I don't know if her visit was standard procedure at the hospital or news station, but my parents don't recall anyone asking permission for a reporter to interview me.

My family and friends had told me the local news stations were widely reporting my story. But interview *me*? I didn't understand why everyone was making such a big deal about what had happened.

My gut reaction was to decline her request, but I said yes to not appear rude to a stranger.

My hospital room filled with familiar faces. My parents walked in, then Barbara, my brother, and a few friends from school trickled in all wearing "I love Jenny" T-shirts, as they had for several days to show me their support. With a large camera pointed in my direction and an audience, I nervously answered the reporter's questions about what happened with a slight Southern accent, as sometimes happens when I'm tired.

As I reclined with my arms and hands lying lifeless on my abdomen, she asked a question only a detached, professional reporter would ask, "Do you think you're going to get better?"

My mind scrambled for an answer. No one had asked me that directly. I'm not sure I'd even had the courage to ask myself this question yet. I wanted to say I was going to walk again, but I'd heard the odds the doctor had given.

"I know that I'm going to get better, somewhat. I don't know how much better, but . . . I guess that just depends on, well, for one thing, how much God wants me to get better."

My stomach dropped as I mentioned God. My hope in God's ability to heal me clashed with my logical brain. Although I knew that walking again was against the odds, I still *believed* it was possible despite the doctor's prediction.

I couldn't come to terms with—much less explain to the world—the impossible probability that I was permanently paralyzed.

CHAPTER THREE

One night at gymnastics practice when I was in first grade, my coach, Mike, kneeled, looked me in the eyes, and asked, "Do you want to join the team? Do you want to be like Nadia?"

My seven-year-old heart nearly burst with joy.

From the age of three, when I had sat in front of a TV watching a girl named Nadia Comaneci doing gymnastics, I had wanted to be like Nadia. After the 1976 Montreal Olympics, my mom enrolled me in gymnastics and dance classes at the local park district near our Chicago-area home. As I progressed, the teacher recommended I take lessons at a gymnastics club at Gymkhana Gymnastics in Schaumburg, Illinois.

After being invited to join the team, I went to practice five nights a week. My typical day from the time I was seven years old was to come home from school, do homework, eat a snack, practice at the gym for four hours, eat dinner, and go to bed. Not only did I learn how to manage my time at an early age, but as a young gymnast, I recognized that hard work, perseverance, and giving my best effort were needed to accomplish something I desired. Without the discipline I learned in gymnastics, I wouldn't be where I am today.

I had great coaches as well as wonderful friends at gymnastics. I was one of the younger girls and looked up to and admired the older gymnasts. They were only a few years older than me, but at the time, they seemed so grown up. My coaches were supportive and fun. There was no yelling when things didn't go well. I never felt any pressure from my parents about gymnastics. My determination and willingness to put in long hours at the gym came from within.

When I was ten, my family moved to Louisville for Dad's job with the FBI. We asked my coaches about gymnastic clubs in the area. After we heard their recommendation, my parents bought a brick ranch house less than two miles from the gym.

I had a new group of friends at the gym, which is where I met Barbara. But the atmosphere was different. The five-night-a-week schedule stayed the same, but there was more pressure. The tone of voice from the head coach was demanding. There was less encouragement and more emphasis on perfection. During this time, I learned how to push through difficult circumstances, even when it was physically, mentally, or emotionally challenging.

In sixth grade, every time I ran or put the full weight and impact of my body on my feet, it felt like a butcher knife was shoved into my heel. The diagnosis from the orthopedist was Sever's disease, a condition that results in pain and inflammation when the growth plate of the heel grows more quickly than the tendons, muscles, and ligaments. It wouldn't cause any permanent damage, so I pushed through the pain. If I wanted to be a gymnast, there was no other option.

The following year, I injured my right foot while on the balance beam. My foot was so swollen and bruised that my shoe didn't fit and I was limping. But an X-ray didn't show a crack, and I continued practicing with the doctor's permission, mostly because of the pressure I received from my coach. When I returned to the doctor for a follow-up, the X-ray revealed that the bone was, indeed, broken. That meant several weeks off of vault and floor, my two best events, but I still worked out on beam and bars—even with a broken foot.

I struggled not only physically but emotionally, from stress and disappointment. But I wasn't going to let anyone see how I felt. I didn't want to look weak.

However, emotions seep out in other ways. My seventh-grade math teacher came up to me after class one day.

"Is everything all right, Jenny?"

My body stiffened and my stomach dropped at her question. Avoiding her eye contact, I said, "Yeah, I'm fine."

How does she know?

"I just wanted to check. You've never received a C in my class."

As an above-average student, I'd never received a C in any subject at school.

Fear is not a good thing to have in gymnastics, and I had plenty of it on beam. A year later, I reinjured my foot doing the same move. I was holding back and didn't go for the flight series—two backflips in a row—as I should have. My coach yelled at me as I hesitated with fear, which only made me feel more flustered. My hands missed the beam, and my foot smacked the side of the beam, cracking it again.

The physical pain was endurable and healed with time. However, the emotional scars from the yelling and pressure left me battered and bruised.

When the coach was mad at my inability to consistently "stick" a routine, he shouted in front of everyone, "You have a snowball's chance in an oven to make it to regionals."

I stared straight into his eyes, while I tried to figure out what he meant. I pictured a snowball in an oven. It would melt. *Oh. I'm not good enough.*

Instead of giving him the pleasure of knowing how much it hurt to hear that, I suppressed my feelings. I never broke eye contact while he was yelling at me, convinced his words went in one ear and out the other. But I was wrong. I had no idea how much his negative comments, yelling, and demand for perfection would impact me in the years to come.

Along with the pain and injuries, I continued to grow taller. Good gymnasts typically are short and petite. Every time my strength would catch up with my height, I would begin another growth spurt. It was a never-ending battle of maintaining the strength and regaining the center of gravity needed to be a successful gymnast.

Yet I still pushed forward, always trying to improve despite my inability to be at the elite level I had dreamed of when I was younger. I was never going to be Nadia or Mary Lou Retton. In gymnastics, I strived to be the best I could be. But it's difficult when your best isn't good enough.

When I was in eighth grade, the coach was working with—

what seemed to some of us—his favorites. Barbara had once been in that group, despite her willingness to talk back to him, which I envied. But she had fallen from his good graces for some reason. Barbara and I, along with a few other gymnasts, practiced on the uneven bars without supervision or input. That evening, the years of being on the receiving end of this behavior came to a head. I don't recall discussing it, but Barbara and I grabbed our floor music and walked out of the gym in the middle of practice. That act of defiance was, in essence, a letter of resignation. It still blows my mind that as thirteen- and four-teen-year-olds we made that decision on our own.

But we weren't finished with gymnastics. After checking out two other gyms, we settled on one and began another year of competition. There was less stress, and it was a better experience since we could enjoy the sport again without a high level of external pressure. Although I still didn't qualify for regionals that year, I did have a few solid competitions. At one of those meets, I qualified for the Junior Olympics.

When I was fourteen, Barbara and I walked side-by-side into the Carrier Dome with a contingent of Kentucky athletes during the opening ceremonies for the 1987 AAU Junior Olympics in Syracuse, New York. We were among a handful of gymnasts who qualified from the state for the national competi-tion. I proudly wore the T-shirt I received in the welcome package full of goodies upon our arrival. I paired the shirt with my only pair of Guess jeans and my Tretorn sneakers.

Thousands of onlookers roared and clapped as each state was announced over the sound system. The stadium held hundreds of competitors from dozens of sports. I soaked in the cheers along with the buzz of excitement generated by the athletes. I knew this was the closest I would ever get to the Olympics, and my insides fluttered with nerves at the opportunity to compete in a national competition.

As with all competitions, I rarely did as well as I performed during practice. My nerves always got the better of me. But on beam, I didn't fall, which was as close to perfection as I could get. Near the end of my one minute and thirty seconds on the beam, I took a deep breath, put the full weight of my body on my left leg, stretched my right leg behind me, extended my arms above me, arching my back. I swung my right leg and threw a gainer layout—a backflip with no hands. My right foot, then my left, made solid contact with the beam. A smile lit up my face as I finished the move in flare, my head held high and arms extended elegantly to the tips of my fingers. It was the first time I had attempted the skill in competition. I stuck it.

In the video from this competition, you see Barbara on a metal folding chair. As I prepared for the gainer, she stood up, hands clasped together with worry. She jumped up and down with delight as I landed. After I completed the routine, I slowly walked to the seating area until I saw Barbara. We ran toward each other, hugging in mutual joy at a successful routine.

I didn't know it at the time, but that was my last gymnastics competition.

Barbara decided to leave competitive gymnastics several months later. I didn't understand her reason for quitting, but I later learned Barbara, who always seemed fearless, had been experiencing more anxiety as she learned more difficult skills.

However, I wanted to stay at the gym, even if it was without my closest friend by my side. I told the coach I wanted to take a year off of competition, which was unheard of. Still growing taller and my body changing as I matured, I needed time to build strength and improve the difficultly of my routines. I also needed a break from the stress of competition.

He said, "Compete or quit."

I quit.

~

After I left competitive gymnastics in ninth grade, I suddenly had twenty hours of "free" time each week. Word got around that I was no longer competing, and a few weeks later the owner of a local gym called me.

"Jenny, would you be interested in coaching with us?" she asked.

With butterflies in my stomach, I answered, "Yes."

Coaching! And a real job paying $3.75 an hour.

I jumped up and down around my bedroom in anticipation of continuing in the sport I loved, albeit in a different capacity.

A few months before my fifteenth birthday, I started working at Kentucky Gymnastics Academy. From my own experience, I wanted to be an encourager, not a mouthpiece of pessimism and defeat. I wanted each girl to know her best was good enough. Being a supportive coach fulfilled me in a way I hadn't expected.

As a coach, I had the opportunity to impart the lessons I had learned in gymnastics: the value of hard work and perseverance in the midst of fear or frustration. I encouraged the girls to always give their best effort, even when they were tired or scared, or just wanted to give up. While I taught these lessons to the gymnasts, I didn't know I would soon have to put them into practice in my own life in ways I had never imagined.

CHAPTER FOUR

"**G**ood night, Jen," my mom said as she left me alone my first night at rehab, after staying with me every night in the hospital. "Are you sure you'll be okay?" I heard the emotion in her voice. Family members weren't allowed to spend the night at rehab.

"Mm-hmm," was all I responded. I didn't want to speak. I felt fear and helplessness creeping in for the first time.

After two and a half weeks at Kosair Children's Hospital, I was transferred to Baptist Hospital East Rehab where I would learn how to adapt to life with a spinal cord injury. After my mom left, I cried as I tried to fall asleep. I was propped on my side with pillows behind my back to keep me positioned comfortably in the hospital bed. Tasting my salty tears, I attempted to wipe them away or move the pillow to a dry spot, but I couldn't move my arms enough to do either. Although I could pull my arms close to my body using my biceps, they were still weak and clumsy.

It's a myth that all quadriplegics have no use of their arms. Some people with more severe injuries can't use their arms at all, while other quads have limited use of their arms, wrists, or hands. I could use my shoulders within days of my injury. Two weeks after my accident, I was able to move my left arm just enough to scratch my nose while I sat in the hospital bed. Oh, that first time scratching my nose was a celebration, indeed! But my hands were useless. My wrists flopped when I moved my arms. If I pulled my arms close to my chest in a fetal position to sleep, I couldn't straighten them out again.

Lying in bed that night, under the weight of the sheet and a light blanket, I felt as swaddled as a baby. As light as the blanket was, it restricted the little movement I had. Beside me was a large call button if I needed assistance from the staff. I hoped I'd be able to scoot or flop my left arm onto the button if I needed help, as I had practiced with my mom before she left.

I finally dozed off, but hospital staff woke me and turned me every two hours throughout the night to prevent pressure sores. I kept my eyes shut, hoping I wouldn't wake up more than necessary. As the sun started to rise, a nurse turned on the blinding fluorescent light and said, "It's time to cath."

I groaned.

Damage to the spinal cord affects not only the movement of limbs but also other bodily functions, such as bladder and bowel. I was just beginning to realize that a spinal cord injury affected every part of my body. Being a sixteen-year-old with the inability to control my bladder and bowels was mortifying.

To empty my bladder, every four to six hours a nurse used a catheter. She folded down the blanket and sheet, removed the pillows, and turned me onto my back. While I looked at the decorated walls, filled with well-wishes from friends and family and even strangers, the nurse bent my knees and opened up my legs. I couldn't feel her cathing me, but the humiliation was suffocating. Everything I had taken for granted—my freedom and independence, and even the ability to go to the bathroom —had been stripped away.

With assistance from several nurses, I was given a sponge bath, then dressed in shorts. While I was still on my back, one of them tugged a large, loose T-shirt from my favorite Christian rock band White Heart over my head and neck brace. I'd bought the T-shirt at one of their concerts. Barbara and I were not just fans but groupies, attending any White Heart concert within a few hours' drive of Louisville. Wearing the T-shirt brought a sense of normalcy after spending two weeks in a hospital gown.

One side at a time, the nurse gently pulled each arm through the sleeves of my shirt. It was like watching someone else's body; I could see the nurse grasping my wrist, but I had little feeling in my arms. The nurse told me I needed to wear white thigh high support hose to prevent blood clots and keep my blood pressure up. She slid the support hose up my legs, though I couldn't see or feel what she was doing. I stared at the ceiling, counting the tiny dark spots in the ceiling tiles—a pastime I would use frequently to escape reality during the next two months of rehab.

On the count of three, two staff grabbed the sheet under my body and lifted me into a wheelchair with a headrest that allowed me to recline at a comfortable 110-degree angle. Between my low blood pressure and neck brace, I couldn't sit up straight, but I could see my room and the staff pretty well.

A nursing assistant carried in a breakfast tray. She removed the lid to the hot breakfast, droplets of condensation dripping from its edges. "Would you like butter and jelly on your toast?"

"Yes, please."

I had relied on family and friends to help me eat and drink at the hospital. It was a relief to have someone there to help since I hadn't thought about how I would eat without family or friends around me.

She opened the small plastic containers of butter and jelly, spreading each on the bread. She brought the bread to my mouth, and I took a bite. I chewed and swallowed carefully, knowing I needed to be cautious since I couldn't cough well; my injury paralyzed the muscles that helped me cough. The nursing assistant put a straw in a small carton of milk, just like the ones in the school cafeteria. She held it up to my lips for me to take a sip. Eating breakfast was a slow process.

After breakfast, it was already time for therapy. I realized there would be no makeup or styling my hair. Getting dressed and into the wheelchair took time. Plus, Barbara wasn't there to do my makeup, as she had on several occasions. You'd think other more important things would be on my mind, but I was still a sixteen-year-old girl who wanted to look nice. Hair and makeup had been a regular part of my morning routine.

I'm embarrassed to admit that throughout my freshman and sophomore years of high school, I wrote down what outfit I wore to school each day. With the money I'd saved from coaching and babysitting, I purchased two pairs of Guess jeans and paired them with a few different shirts and sweaters, trying not to repeat the same combination in a one- or two-week period. Then I'd do my makeup: Cover Girl foundation, powder, and blush; Avon blue eyeliner; and blue mascara. Yes, even blue mascara to match my bright blue eyes. The look was always finished off with pink shimmery lipstick.

I'd set my fine blonde hair, lightened naturally by the summer sun, in hot rollers while I dressed and put on my makeup. Then I'd take out the rollers, shake my head upside down, and use the fruity-smelling Aussie hairspray in hopes the curl and body would hold at least halfway through the day. My curling iron and more hairspray finished off the "big bangs" look of the late 1980s. The process of doing my hair took a full half hour.

Shorts, T-shirt, support hose, no makeup or styled hair was anything but my definition of a fashion statement. But it was time for therapy. I was nervous since I didn't know what to expect from physical or occupational therapy. I didn't even know what occupational therapy was.

Twice a day I was going to have PT and OT. I needed to relearn everything: how to sit, how to roll over, how to push a wheelchair, how to brush my teeth, brush my hair, hold a fork to feed myself, pick up a cup to drink. How would I get in and out of a wheelchair using only my arms when those arms had very limited function? Could I get dressed by myself? So many questions were going through my head.

An assistant pushed my wheelchair into the gym filled with therapy mats, weights, and parallel bars to practice walking. Mostly older people shuffled around the gym with the assistance of walkers, a therapist by their side. I looked around and noticed I was the youngest patient by a decade or two. This was where I was supposed to learn how to live my new life.

I met Mark, a physical therapy student. He had a stocky build, brown hair, and a mustache and wore a white lab coat, tie, gray pants, and a red name badge pinned to his coat. He seemed kind and friendly. Looking back, I think he was every bit as nervous as I was.

"We're going to get you onto the mat. Have you used a sliding board before?"

"No."

He showed me a plastic board, twenty-six inches long by eight inches wide.

"We're going to put the transfer board under your bottom, then slide you over to the therapy mat. Sound good?"

I wasn't sure it sounded good, but it seemed like it was what I needed to do.

He moved my wheelchair next to the mat, which was the same height as my chair, and removed the armrest of the chair. Mark gently lifted my right leg and slipped the board under my thigh.

"I'm going to bring your upper body forward. I've got you, okay?"

"Mm-hmm," I answered nervously.

While supporting my upper body, he grabbed my hips and slid me over the sliding board and onto the mat. With one hand holding my shoulder to keep me upright, he pulled the board out from under me with the other.

That was easier than I expected.

But I still didn't like the lack of control I felt. I'd been used to telling my body to work against gravity for years. Now other people—nurses, assistants, and therapists—were moving my body for me.

The first day on the therapy mat while lying on my back, I started with simple exercises. Mark placed half-pound weights around my wrists. I used the few muscles I could: my shoulders, biceps, and wrists. After an hour of therapy, I was exhausted.

In occupational therapy, Val focused on activities of daily living, such as eating and brushing my teeth. She gave me a universal cuff that I slid around the palm of my hand. The cuff had a small pocket into which I inserted my fork or toothbrush, allowing me to practice small, but significant, everyday tasks. Val had me work with weights as well.

Sometimes those half-pound weights seemed to laugh at me, chiding me for being so weak physically. Slowly a half-pound increased to a one-pound weight; one pound became two pounds. It was a time to celebrate the little things.

Each day Mark taught me new skills. I learned to sit on the mat with my arms at my sides for stability. Since I had no use of my stomach or back muscles to keep me upright, the position of my arms and head controlled my entire body. I got the hang of this pretty quickly. My strong sense of balance from gymnastics helped, and I easily found my center of gravity and tested the limits of my stability when Mark had me lift my arms off the mat or lean forward.

Using the momentum of my swinging arms, I practiced rolling over on the mat. As the swelling in my spinal cord decreased, I began to regain a bit more use of some muscles in my wrists and continued strengthening my arms. I still couldn't lift my arms above my head without them crashing down. My fingers remained lifeless.

Mark also stretched each of my legs up and down and side to side for range of motion exercises to keep my muscles flexible. I had been experiencing severe spasticity—involuntary muscle spasms that occur from wayward messages firing in the spinal cord. The medication my doctor prescribed for the muscle spasms made me drowsy. Unfortunately, my spasms worsened over time.

Even in the ICU, my fingers would twitch, and my legs would jump involuntarily. At first, the spasms gave me hope that I was getting better. I figured the spasms were a good sign I was going to be able to walk again. But the spasms were often strong enough to take my breath away or unexpectedly extend or flex my legs and hips.

At rehab, I also learned to push a new manual chair by myself. Pushing the wheelchair to and from therapy gave me a bit of freedom. In the chair I sat up straight—close to ninety degrees—with a lower backrest that sat at about my shoulder blades. I still wore the uncomfortable neck brace to allow my spinal fusion to heal properly. The push rims on the wheels had projections called "quad knobs" that I pushed to slowly make my way through the halls of the hospital.

In physical therapy, I discovered that my years in gymnastics paid off not only with my balance but in my ability to push through pain and frustration. I approached PT with the same determination and hard work that I had approached gymnastics. Therapy was just another workout. Difficult, slowly progressing workouts.

Several weeks into my stay at rehab, I was sitting in my room after PT and OT finished for the day. The bright sun warmed the hospital room, which always felt cold to me. I still wore a pair of shorts, a T-shirt, and those dreaded compression stockings. At least I got to wear my high-top Reebok cheerleading sneakers. And the nurses now pulled my hair up into a high ponytail to keep it out of my face during therapy. Sometimes I even asked for my signature pastel pink lipstick. The shoes, ponytail, and lipstick gave me a sense of familiarity in this new world. I don't recall anyone else being in the room with me that afternoon, although I was rarely alone since my friends were still out of school for the summer. A nurse poked her head in and told me I had a visitor.

As I turned toward the door, a woman using a wheelchair entered my room. She was in her twenties and had short, curly hair with natural shades of blonde, brown, and a hint of red. Her wheelchair was sportier than mine. I noticed she had no quad knobs, yet easily propelled her chair into my room without assistance, even though her hands were limp and lifeless, just like mine.

"Hi, Jenny. My name is Lois."

This was the first time I met a person with a spinal cord injury. I was the only patient with a spinal cord injury at the rehab hospital. Social media didn't exist to connect with others online, and there was no YouTube to watch how a quadriplegic could transfer into bed or brush their teeth. I was glued to every word she said, wanting to learn as much as possible.

"Five years ago, I fell off a ladder and broke my neck," Lois began. "I played basketball, volleyball, and softball in college and got a degree in biology before my injury. I was almost finished with a nursing degree when my accident happened. I finally finished nursing school two years after my injury." Her voice was full of hope and determination.

Part of me felt encouraged by Lois's story. She finished college. She could even drive. But another side of me sat there disheartened. She hadn't gotten better.

I don't think I spoke ten words the whole time Lois was with me. Still, I soaked in every word she said, especially when she showed me a trick that quadriplegics use called tenodesis. She explained that tenodesis happens when a quad extends their wrist muscles, which causes the fingers and thumb to naturally close into a loose grip. (Try it. Relax your wrist and let it drop down. Keep your fingers relaxed—don't get tempted to use them—and pull your wrist up. Watch what your fingers and thumb do.)

Lois demonstrated how she could pick up items as small as a coin off the floor using tenodesis. She pulled a pen out of her purse and arranged it between her thumb, first finger, and middle finger. She wrote her name and laid the pen on the hospital tray table.

"Go ahead. Try it," she said optimistically.

Mimicking her actions, I held the pen in my weak right hand. I tried writing my name on a piece of paper. My hand wobbled. My handwriting, in which I used to take pride, was barely decipherable.

Next Lois pulled a tube of mascara with a small splint attached to it from her purse. She quickly had my full attention. Using her teeth to hold the tube and the palms of both hands on the lid, Lois twisted open the mascara. She showed me how she applied mascara using the splint that held her fingers on the wand.

I was a sixteen-year-old girl who wanted to wear a cute outfit, style my hair, and look pretty. That tube of mascara gave me hope. It gave me a glimpse of applying my makeup without assistance. But more importantly, through Lois, God was showing me His plans to give me "hope and a future" (Jer. 29:11 NIV).

Lois also talked about practical, personal concerns about managing her bladder.

I still needed to be catheterized every four to six hours. My doctor's goal was for my bladder to hold urine until the small rubber tube, called a catheter, could be inserted through the urethra to drain my bladder of urine. However, even my bladder had spasms, causing embarrassing accidents.

Lois explained that she used a Foley catheter, or indwelling catheter, since catheterizing independently as a female quadriplegic was impossible for her. She didn't want to be dependent on someone to go to the bathroom. A few days after Lois's visit, I discussed the option of managing my bladder with a Foley catheter with my doctor. We decided to try it.

The next day, a nurse placed a Foley catheter into my bladder and kept it in place by inflating a small balloon with saline. Once the catheter was in place, she attached a small collection bag for urine, which I placed near my hip under my underwear, just like Lois showed me. From then on, instead of getting in bed every four hours, undressing, and being catheterized by a nurse, I simply emptied the bag into the toilet with assistance. What had taken a half hour took just minutes. It was another small victory.

Worse than figuring out my bladder was managing my bowels. Pooping was now a daily topic that involved nurses, doctors, and even my mom. Yes, everyone poops, but not everyone talks about pooping.

I soon gained an in-depth knowledge of what a "bowel program" is.

The goal for my bowel program was to train my body to go only on command. As we tried the program the first time, a nurse inserted a suppository while I was lying on my side in bed, then the staff got me onto a commode chair next to my hospital bed. With little support to keep my balance, I felt my blood pressure drop, just like when I went from my bed to my wheelchair.

"Please, get me into bed. I'm going to faint." I panicked as my vision blacked out and I could barely hear the nurses reassuring me I was all right over the sound of rushing wind in my ears.

I am not *all right.*

I'd never come close to passing out in my life before my injury. Within a few minutes, my blood pressure came back up. I didn't fall or pass out, but the experience left me terrified. After that night, I refused to do the bowel program sitting up. Instead, I stayed on my side with a disposable pad to hold the poop until the nurses cleaned me up.

I was supposed to go home from rehab in two months, so a

nurse taught my mom how to do my bowel care. Three nights a week, I lay on my side and stared at the hospital wall. I heard the nurse explain to my mom how to insert the suppository. After a half hour or forty-five minutes, the nurse showed her how to do digital stimulation (or "dig stim"), which relaxes the anal sphincter and allows the poop to move freely. Although I could always hear what was going on, I would disassociate. My body was present, but my mind was anywhere but there. The only way I could deal with the indignity of the situation was to not deal with it.

I was lying on a teal blue mat on the far side of the PT gym under a large window. I was on my stomach. On my left, I could hear another physical therapist instructing an elderly patient how to safely use a walker to climb the five wooden steps placed in the corner. Mark was guiding me through some new exercises. I enjoyed being on my stomach, stretching my long body to its full length. But in reality, I could do very little in that position. My neck, now in a soft collar, was weak from being immobilized for so long. Lifting my head to even peek at the wall in front of me was difficult.

Mark asked me if I could try a push-up. In my past life, these were a breeze. I would repeat multiple sets of twenty-five or fifty during conditioning at the end of every gymnastics prac-tice. I moved my hands near my chest and pushed down on the mat. But now, nothing moved. I tried again. My muscles didn't twitch with any sign of movement.

What had once been so simple was now impossible. And that realization devastated me. Suddenly, all my buried feelings came pouring out in tears.

Mark asked, "Is everything okay?"

I just sobbed. It was that kind of crying that can be described only as an ugly cry, where snot ran down my face onto the mat and I gasped for air.

I wasn't okay. But I didn't know what was wrong, much less how I felt or how to express it. Pushing back or hiding the tears was easier. Mark let me lie on the mat until my crying stopped. I rolled over onto my back, able to wipe away the tears that I couldn't four weeks earlier. I took a deep breath.

"Let's get you up in your chair," Mark said. "You've worked hard today."

During rehab, I can honestly say I had fun with my friends in the midst of the chaos. I chatted with my girlfriends and joked around with the guys. But I had no idea how to verbalize what I was going through emotionally.

I was much more of a thinker than a feeler, but I wasn't able to think my way through this situation. My years in gymnastics had taught me how to stuff my feelings, and I never learned from my family how to express my feelings. I also believed a "good Christian" shouldn't be mad at God, though no one ever said or even implied this to me. I didn't want to feel sad. I didn't know how to even express it. I didn't dare allow myself to feel angry at God for letting my accident happen. I hid the sadness, fear, and frustration so I didn't look weak or appear as if I lacked faith in God. I showed my happy face, which *was* genuine the majority of the time. But when I struggled, I didn't share it with my friends or allow others to see it. This only reinforced the "You're so strong" comments I received. It was a vicious cycle.

Before my injury, I had found ways to compensate for my inability to express emotion through a good workout or bike ride or playing piano.

When I was six years old, my next-door neighbor began giving me piano lessons. As I progressed in gymnastics, my time for piano lessons diminished, but my love of playing did not. I started piano lessons again after I quit gymnastics in ninth grade, but my love of music grew into more than playing piano.

In tenth grade, a friend told me that her brother was in a band, and they were looking for a keyboardist. That's how I became a member of Captive, a Christian rock band. I was shy around the guys in the band at first but slowly opened up. Growing up in gymnastics, I was always around girls. Boys were scary. But Kevin, Scott, and David became great friends. Among my friends and family, they were collectively known as "the guys."

Scott usually picked me up for practice in his old blue Chevrolet Chevette. We practiced at a small church twice a week. Three amplifiers and the church's sound system blasted rock music up to the church rafters . . . and beyond. The neighbors eventually asked us to keep the noise down. The guys loved to laugh and joke around, and all of us loved rock music.

Soon after I arrived at rehab, the guys showed up in my room and told me they were ready to have band practice. David squeezed several pieces of his drum set into one corner, while Kevin and Scott plugged in their bass and electric guitars and my keyboard into amplifiers.

The only problem was I couldn't use my fingers to play piano or keyboard anymore.

The guys weren't going to let a little thing like that stop us.

Kevin left my room and returned with tape from the nurses' station. Grabbing a toothbrush, he taped it to my index finger.

(I'm not sure what his theory behind this was, but I went along with it.) I tried pressing my finger on a key using the toothbrush as leverage with no success. After many failed attempts at modifying me or the equipment, I finally figured out I could use the side of each hand or my thumbs to press down on the keys. I wasn't able to play chords, but I could still play in the band with the guys.

Closing the door of my room, Kevin and Scott tuned their instruments.

"One, two, three, four . . ." David counted.

Scott began playing his guitar, Kevin came in on his bass and lead vocals, then David and I joined in as we played a cover of a song by Petra. Although the volume on the amps was turned down low, the entire rehab wing was audience to a rock concert.

A couple of local bands, Bride and Spanky Lee, offered to host a benefit concert to raise money for my medical expenses. They even invited our band to play at the concert. Kevin decided to name the event "JennyRock." I'm serious. With great anticipation—and deafening the hospital hallways in the process—we practiced to play in front of an audience of a thousand at Memorial Auditorium in downtown Louisville.

With this concert, a basketball benefit game between former University of Louisville and University of Kentucky basketball players, and students who participated in "Jump Rope for Jenny" at Norton Elementary School, thousands of dollars were raised for my medical expenses. It was the 1980s version of GoFundMe.

Several years later, I stopped by to visit the nurses and my therapists. One of the nurses mused, "It was so quiet after you left."

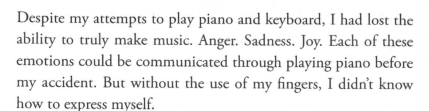

Despite my attempts to play piano and keyboard, I had lost the ability to truly make music. Anger. Sadness. Joy. Each of these emotions could be communicated through playing piano before my accident. But without the use of my fingers, I didn't know how to express myself.

Once my fingers were paralyzed, so was my heart.

CHAPTER FIVE

I had begged my parents to let me go to Christian Academy of Louisville for my freshman year of high school. Despite my pleas, I ended up returning to public school. But just before I started tenth grade, my parents decided I could go to Christian Academy. With eagerness, I began a new school year at the school Barbara attended.

Christian Academy of Louisville was everything my previous high school was not. It was a small school; my sophomore class had just sixteen students. I finally felt a sense of belonging at school. I had great friends and was involved in school activities. I cheered and played volleyball. I was in the Spanish Club and Beta Club. I was even nominated as a homecoming princess. Every girl should get to experience one perfect year of high school as I did.

I got my driver's permit the day after my sixteenth birthday and my license thirty days later. I was so excited that my mom wouldn't have to drive me around anymore. And she was just as relieved to no longer act as my chauffeur; she let me drive myself to work as a gymnastics coach, band practice, and church activities.

I was independent and free.

But that independence would last only five months.

When my friends returned to school in late August, I was still at the rehab hospital. Each afternoon after I finished therapy, my teachers came to the hospital to tutor me and assign me homework. I attempted to complete my lessons on time as best I could. Keeping up with all of my subjects was challenging. As a visual learner, outlining my textbooks had always helped me study, but I couldn't do this now. Precalculus was the most challenging. How was I supposed to solve a formula when I couldn't write out the steps of the equation? Without the ability to write quickly or legibly, it was difficult to complete my assignments to my standards of perfection.

In mid-September, as part of my rehab program, I returned to school for two classes a day on campus, which was about three miles from the hospital. The first morning, the nursing staff dressed and transferred me into my manual wheelchair, while an assistant brought a breakfast tray to the room.

"Can you open the milk and straw?" I asked. The assistant opened both for me.

"Do you need anything else?"

I looked around the room. Everything I needed was within reach. "No, thanks."

I reached for the universal cuff—the elastic band with a pocket that held my fork. I scooted the cuff onto the palm of my right hand, then grasped the fork from the table using tenodesis. I placed the prongs of the fork into my mouth.

(Teeth are a quad's best assistive device.) I held it tightly between my teeth and pushed the fork into the sleeve of the pocket of the universal cuff.

Got it!

My hand was still wobbly and weak, but I ate breakfast without assistance. I didn't mind that half my scrambled eggs ended up in my lap. I placed the milk carton between the heel of each hand and picked up the milk and sipped it with a straw.

After breakfast, I pushed the food tray to the side and pulled my makeup close. Val, my occupational therapist, had closely examined the splint Lois used with her mascara on the day of her visit. Within a few days, she made personalized splints for my blush brush and mascara, which allowed me to apply my makeup without help. Each new activity I learned gave me a sense of accomplishment, but I longed for the days when I could turn off my alarm, shower, dress, and eat without anyone's help.

I couldn't do my hair, and I wore a T-shirt, sweatpants, and tennis shoes, which were against the dress code. I returned to school with anticipation and uncertainty. I was excited to be with my friends outside of the hospital. But what would be different?

My grandma drove me to school in the used Ford Econoline van with a wheelchair lift that my dad had purchased. A few classmates met me in the parking lot and pushed me to class.

"There's a step into Mr. Greschel's room," a friend mentioned.

I looked around the small campus with new eyes. The square courtyard was bordered with a walkway where our lockers were sheltered by an overhang that provided little protection from the elements. Several dogwood trees grew in the grassy area in the courtyard. On two opposing sides of the courtyard, the doors to six classrooms each had a single step, mocking my presence. On the far side of the square, the cafeteria, office, and several more classrooms also were up one step. To my left was the gym. It, too, had a step.

Ugh. Why are steps even needed?

We rolled my chair a few feet to Mr. Greschel's room for history class.

"Tip the wheelchair backward to get the front casters up onto the step," I instructed Mark as I steadied myself by wrapping my wrists under the armrests of my chair. "Now lift the back of the wheelchair and push me in."

After moving my chair between two desks in the first row, I awkwardly flipped open a notebook that rested on top of the two textbooks on my lap.

"Can you take the lid off my pen?" I asked Mark.

He carefully handed me the pen, and I placed the roller ball into a hole in the adaptive pen holder Val gave me to practice writing. I slid the device onto the palm of my hand that secured my pointer finger above the pen with a piece of metal.

We settled in, and history class began. Using minuscule movements of my shoulder and bicep, I attempted to take notes. Whether I could read my writing when I returned to the hospital is a matter of debate.

When the bell rang after fifty minutes, my arm was tired.

As we left the classroom, we reversed the process of going into a room: Mark rolled my wheelchair backward while holding onto the push handles on the back of the chair and guided the large wheels down the step, then continued to pull the chair backward until the front casters were safely on the ground.

What was usually a short walk to my next class seemed an impossible distance. As I slowly pushed my chair around the courtyard, I noticed the concrete sloped to the right and gravity pulled my chair down the slant. It forced me to push more with my right arm to keep the chair going straight. I stopped halfway to catch a breath and rest my cramped arms. My friends offered to help. I refused.

I have to learn to do this by myself.

I was grateful they were willing to help, but my stubbornness and desire for independence outweighed the temporary ease of accepting a push.

I started to move toward the door again, then went up the step with assistance and wheeled into Junior English with Mrs. Record. She still seemed ancient as dirt. During class she drilled grammar and fed us literature. I must have looked tired because a classmate offered to share her notes with me. I shook my head no like a two-year-old saying, "I do it by myself!" and continued to write in my notebook, determined to take my *own* notes.

By the end of two classes, I was worn out. My arms ached, and my brain was tired. The chance to be at school made life feel a little bit more normal, but I hadn't expected to need so much help.

In the back of the van as we returned to rehab, I wondered, *Is life always going to be this difficult?*

As part of recreational therapy, I also went out with friends and family around town.

One evening after therapy and dinner, my mom drove Barbara and me to the mall. With that awful neck brace and my mom walking nearby, I pushed my wheelchair over the marble tile.

"I feel like everyone is looking at me," I whispered to Barbara. Children and adults stared as they recognized me from the stories on the local news stations.

One little kid ran up to me and asked, "Are you that cheerleader?"

I rolled my eyes and wanted to say, "Gymnast, not cheerleader." But I simply nodded my head as best I could within the confines of the neck brace. The girl ran back to her mother, who looked embarrassed about her daughter's curiosity. Feeling more self-conscious than ever, I pushed into The Limited and hid from the world between the racks of clothing.

Soon after I returned to school, the hospital staff also allowed me to go to church. My mom arrived at rehab early Sunday to help me put on a trendy black floral drop-waist dress and pantyhose, my normal apparel at the time for a Sunday morning at church. That was the first—and the last—time after my injury that I ever wore pantyhose. I wanted to blend in as much as possible with everyone, pretend that nothing had changed for a few hours.

After rolling, pulling, tugging, turning, and transferring into the chair, I was upset with how the dress looked in a seated position. The material bunched up in a muddled heap in my lap, while at the same time it pulled tightly over my abdomen. The dress also sat too short on my long legs. I put on my makeup but criticized my mom when she tried styling my hair.

"Not like *that*, Mom. Do it like Barbara does," I snapped. But I couldn't show or explain how to do the big bangs that were in style.

With both of us frazzled and irritated, my mom loaded me

in the van, and we rode in silence the twenty minutes to church.

We had attended Northeast Christian, a church of about 250 people since we moved to Louisville when I was eleven. I was part of the youth group in middle and high school and played piano during church services.

After reuniting with friends for a few minutes before the service started, my mom took a seat in a wooden upholstered chair on the aisle. I maneuvered my wheelchair next to her. I was sitting in the middle aisle of the church in full view of everyone. At least it felt that way.

The pastor said, "Everyone, please stand."

Huh, I thought. I looked up at my mom and chuckled. "Well, I hadn't even thought about that!"

In mid-October, just a week from my discharge from rehab, I prepared for another excursion. A few girlfriends came to my room after school. I let Barbara do my makeup and style my hair with hot rollers, a curling iron, and enough aerosol hairspray to destroy the earth's environment. We piled into the van, and my mom drove us downtown for a concert by Richard Marx, a pop-rock ballad singer.

When we ordered the tickets, we asked for seating for a wheelchair. All of us squealed when we saw our floor-level seats in the front half of Louisville Gardens. I sat at the end of a row, but as the music exploded through the sound system, my stomach sank with disappointment when the crowd rose and cheered. My view of the stage was completely obstructed while the cheering fans stood and sang along with the music. This was my first of a lifetime of events with "butt-view" seating.

Despite my limited view, my girlfriends and I were still giddy when we arrived back at rehab after midnight. We found the doors to the rehab side of the hospital were locked. Our only way in was through the emergency room. We laughed as we explained our predicament to the ER staff, who were confused about why a patient had been out so late—or at all.

～

With butterflies in my stomach, I was discharged from rehab in mid-October. We packed up my room and left the walls bare. I said my goodbyes to the nursing staff but knew I'd be back several days a week for outpatient therapy.

It was the first time since my injury that I'd been home, despite the opportunities I'd had to leave rehab. The house looked basically the same as it had two and a half months ago. My dad pushed me up the new wooden ramp constructed at the front door. Thankfully, the house was only one story with a basement, which meant I'd have access to my bedroom and the hall bathroom. At least that's what I expected.

I groaned as I attempted to push through the narrow hallway covered in thick carpet. My dad stepped in and pushed my chair down the hall. We passed my brother's room on the left, the bathroom on the right, my parents' room on the right, and finally my bedroom at the end of the hall. Other than the freshly painted walls similar in color to the pale green I'd previously had, there was no sign a teenage girl had ever lived there. I stared at my room in horror.

"Where is all my stuff?" I said in disbelief.

In preparing for my homecoming and the new hospital bed, the room had been stripped bare. Anything nonessential was removed to provide more space for my chair and whoever would help me with personal care. The colorful collage of favorite quotes and sayings, which had taken me years to create, had been removed from the back of my bedroom door. Posters of my favorite bands and musicians had disappeared.

"We needed to clean and make room for the hospital bed."

"But . . ."

My sanctuary was gone. All I had wanted was to return to the familiarity of home, but everything familiar had disappeared.

As if my bedroom weren't enough, I discovered I couldn't get into the bathroom. My wheelchair barely squeaked through the doorframe, but there wasn't enough space to turn to reach the sink, the toilet, or the shower. I wasn't going to be able to brush my teeth or wash my face in the bathroom. A shower was out of the question. I was completely dependent on others.

Coming home made my injury more real. Rehab was a safe environment, isolating me from the reality of my new life. Returning home accentuated the changes that had occurred.

It wasn't just my bedroom that had changed.

My fourteen-year-old brother Matthew seemed absent from the house. We had fought like cats and dogs, and he can show you scars from my fingernails to prove it. He was a bratty little brother, and I confess that I was a bossy, know-it-all older sister. Now that I was home again, we didn't argue like we used to. He'd been lost in the shuffle and immediately became responsible for doing his laundry, ironing, and other household chores because my parents were busy working and caring for me.

Several years ago, I asked Matthew how my injury affected him.

"I got away with some serious crap during that time!" he said. His lighthearted response gave me a bit of relief since I always felt I'd ruined his life to some extent. My parents wouldn't let him play football because it was "too dangerous," and he wasn't allowed to drive until he was seventeen. In that same conversation, Matthew admitted that when I returned home, he would purposely place the TV remote out of my reach or leave his shoes in the middle of the floor, preventing me from pushing my chair to where I needed to go. Well, one thing hadn't changed: Matthew was still my little brother.

When I returned home, my mom had to help me bathe and dress for school, while she got herself ready to go to her job as a bookkeeper at Norton Elementary School. She had returned to work when I entered rehab two and a half weeks after my injury since our health insurance was through her job. When she returned in the evening, she helped me get ready for and into bed, which included the time-consuming bowel program.

My dad returned to his job as an FBI agent in the Louisville field office. He had also become the spokesperson for the family during television interviews. With both my mom and dad working, plus the added responsibility of caring for me, my parents were barely surviving.

One evening while my mom was helping me get undressed, she burst into tears.

"I'm sorry, Jen," she said and quickly left my room to collect herself.

I lay there confused and helpless, lost in my thoughts.

It's because of me Mom is sad.

And though I didn't think it was my fault, I still felt responsible.

My grandma, Betty Carter, had seen the need for additional support and made the decision—at the age of sixty-five—to sell her home in Arizona and move in with us. We had a finished basement and it became her residence for the next fifteen years. She not only drove me to school, but took over the responsibility of getting me up each morning for the next several years, freeing my mom in the morning. It was Grandma's job to help me go to the bathroom at school.

Returning home also meant returning to school full-time. After third period in the building where the library was located, I pushed as stealthily as possible to the janitor's closet to meet my grandma.

"Hi, hon," she greeted me as I tried to invisibly enter the janitor's closet. The bathroom was inaccessible, so this was the only accommodation the school had found for us.

"Hey, Grandma."

While my grandma opened an empty Sprite bottle, I pulled the small collection bag out from its hiding place inside my underwear at my hip. Making sure the four-inch extension tube was in the bottle, she pulled the lever up, and urine flowed from the bag. After she closed the valve, I tucked the bag back inside my underwear like I was hiding a dirty little secret. Grandma put the lid back on the warm Sprite bottle.

When we were done, I left the closet and went to the cafeteria with the help of a friend, down one step out of one building, then up one step to the cafeteria where I'd have lunch. Throughout the day, I limited how much I drank so I wouldn't need to meet my grandma more than once a day. It just wasn't cool having your grandma help you pee.

By the beginning of 1990—four months after my return home —the Home Builders Association of Louisville had turned our garage into a fully accessible bedroom suite for me and built an accessible family/study room. They volunteered their time and talents, while my parents paid for the building materials. The carpeting in most of the house was replaced with wood floors that made it easier to push my chair.

My new bedroom was spacious, with a walk-in closet I could see from my full-size bed. The bathroom had a roll-in shower. I also could fit under the sink and countertops to put on makeup or wash my face and brush my teeth without assistance. Fragments of freedom.

I got to select the flooring and the wallpaper I wanted in my room. My floor had large black and white vinyl tile squares, and one wall was decorated with wallpaper with lines of musical notes. Red was my accent color with a red coverlet for my bed, red rose accents here and there, and red towels in my bathroom.

At the moment of my injury, I had lost control of every area of my life. I doubt anyone realized how grateful I was to make such seemingly insignificant decisions about decorating my room; it gave me a sense of control in one little area of my life.

CHAPTER SIX

Cheerleaders, their families, coaches, and spectators stared at me as I struggled to push my wheelchair through the halls of the Opryland Hotel. Just one year earlier, Barbara, Suzy, another former gymnast, and I had led Christian Academy to win "Best Tumbling Cheerleading Team" at the International Cheerleading Federation's National Championships in Nashville, Tennessee. Six months after my injury, I cheered for my friends from the sidelines.

I wore white sweatpants, a royal blue sweatshirt, and my cheerleading shoes. I'd applied my makeup, and my mom had pulled my hair into a ponytail before we left the hotel room, though I grumbled it was a bit too lumpy. Barbara tied a blue ribbon around my ponytail so I would match the team. But as much as I tried to blend in, I didn't. I couldn't even push my wheelchair through the thick carpet. I remembered the previous year: everyone had oohed and aahed while watching me tumble because I was one of the best. One year later, I wasn't a valuable asset to my team or a respected competitor. I wanted to yell, "You don't know who I am!"

As I neared the door of my hotel room, I breathed a sigh of relief. I just wanted a moment to get away from the curious onlookers. One of my friends helped me unlock the door with the key, but I struggled to push the heavy hotel room door by myself, trying again and again to shove the door open with my footrest as the palms of my hands tried to push my chair forward. The door wouldn't budge.

A dam of emotions broke open. I began crying in front of my friends, which made me feel so much more vulnerable than when I sobbed in front of my physical therapist. But it wasn't about the heavy door. It was about loss. The loss of my ability to walk, the loss of use of my hands, the loss of independence, and—the most painful—the loss of my identity.

Who am I?

The identity I had established throughout my life was gone. The outside world no longer saw me as the gymnast that I was . . . or used to be.

I'm not a gymnast anymore.

A void ruptured in the depths of my soul with that realization.

After a good cry, I fixed my makeup and returned to the competition with my friends and acted as if nothing had happened an hour earlier. I cheered for them. I don't remember if the team did well in the competition, but I do know a small part of me died that afternoon.

Later in the school year, I went to a basketball game at school on a Friday night. I was determined to do everything I had before my injury, and doing the normal activities of a teenage girl gave me a sense of comfort. The gym was crowded and noisy, and I felt as if I was in everyone's way as I sat at the end of the bleachers near the stage, close to the cheerleading squad. At halftime, I lived vicariously through Barbara as I watched her do a tumbling run, although I noticed she wasn't performing the back tucks and layouts she normally did.

"Excuse me," I said to a student. "Excuse me!" I said a bit louder to be heard and pushed my way forward. I moved as close to the court as I could, trying to call Barbara's name as loudly as possible with my limited lung capacity.

"Hey, Barb! Barb!" She turned around. "Will you throw some back tucks or layouts for me?"

She looked at me with a blank stare, shook her head no, turned around, and walked away.

I crinkled my eyebrows in confusion.

Why won't she do something I'd give anything to be able to do again?

At the time I didn't know how much Barbara was suffering from pain and grief. Neither of us had been good communicators despite the amount of time we spent together. We didn't talk about matters of the heart like crushes on boys or the stress of living up to our unrealistically high expectations. Both of us had perfected the art of stuffing our emotions. We never talked about my injury. Life just went on.

I later learned that she was thinking, *I shouldn't be doing this because Jenny can't.*

Gymnastics was the glue that had bound us together. And that was gone.

My friendship with Barbara lost its spark after my injury. She didn't leave my side, but our lives were no longer intertwined in the way they had been. We no longer spent hours together at cheerleading and volleyball practice. I couldn't spend the night at her house, and we didn't swim in her pool on long summer days. We no longer walked to the neighborhood pool, hoping to catch a glimpse of the cute guys from the local Catholic high school.

I often hear people who have sustained injuries say their friends abandoned them after their injury. I wasn't abandoned. But I did feel left behind as my friends, including Barbara, started making plans to go away to college, while I planned to go to a local university and live at home—dependent on others for my daily needs.

I may have lost my physical independence and my identity as a gymnast, but I poured every ounce of time and effort into being a great student. *That* I could do. Eager to graduate early with my friends who were seniors, I spent the rest of the school year in the library during my free period, working on an independent study course for the only class I needed to graduate early: Senior English. Reading literature was difficult enough, but I had to fight to stay awake because of the drowsiness caused by the medication for my muscle spasms. However, I finished the course on time and was graduating.

The graduation ceremony was at a local seminary. In front of the chapel's large white columns and tall steeple, the senior class of twenty-six students had our picture taken. Against my wishes but out of necessity, my hair was cut shorter and permed since neither my hands—nor my mom's—could successfully operate the hot rollers, curling iron, and hairspray. I hated that a spinal cord injury had robbed me of so much, even my hair.

Wearing a white cap and gown, as well as my trademark pink lipstick and blue eyeliner and mascara, I stopped outside the chapel while a local news station interviewed me. I was getting used to the interviews, but I was frustrated by the attention. I sarcastically told the reporter, "I just want to graduate like everyone else." In the news story, it was used as an "inspirational" quote, but what I was trying to say was "please leave me alone."

In the chapel, my concern wasn't focused on the five steps that impeded my way to the stage to receive my diploma. By this time, I was comfortable with being carried in my wheelchair up and down steps, and I trusted two classmates to safely get me onto the stage. My fear was that even a subtle movement while lifting me up the stairs would set off my muscle spasms and make a scene in front of so many people.

I watched other graduates cross the stage until my name was announced with a pause between each word: "Jennifer . . . Lynn . . . Smith." My classmates lifted my chair and carried me step by step onto the stage. I held my breath as my legs tightened and drew up about four inches. I wrapped my arms under the armrests of the chair and attempted to calm my body. Thankfully, my legs relaxed, and I let a small smile of relief light up my face. A friend pushed me across the stage, and Mrs. Weaver placed the diploma in my lap. In the video of the graduation ceremony, the camera panned to the audience, cheering and applauding in a standing ovation.

I did what seemed impossible to me just ten months earlier: I graduated from Christian Academy one year early at the age of seventeen.

CHAPTER SEVEN

I n August 1990, I began taking classes at the University of Louisville. The sprawling campus stood in stark contrast to my small high school. The university had a smattering of Victorian-era buildings, but most of my classes were in buildings from the 1950s, '60s, and '70s. Massive oak, ash, and flowering dogwood trees gave parts of the campus an urban forest vibe, especially with its unique population of white squirrels.

Scott, David, and Steve also enrolled that year as full-time students. Three mornings a week they transferred me into one of their cars, folded my manual chair—now with plastic-coated push rims instead of quad knobs—and placed it in the trunk. UofL was mostly a commuter school at the time with few opportunities for extracurricular activities, so my "college experience" really wasn't anything more than going to classes, studying, and relearning how to write. Oh, and figuring out how to live life in a wheelchair. And discovering the physical barriers that existed on campus.

I was quite dependent on my friends to get around campus with its long, steep ramps, heavy doors, and freight elevators.

The Americans with Disabilities Act—a civil rights law prohibiting discrimination against people with disabilities, which includes access to employment, transportation, and buildings open to the public—had just been signed on July 26, 1990. I had a front-row seat to see how the university would become more accessible over the next eight years.

I started college with no clue about my major. Growing up, I never had an answer for "What do you want to be when you grow up?" So I focused on general education requirements and enjoyed almost all of my classes. I did not like psychology, though. I received a C in Psychology 101 my first semester. I tried to dismiss this "failure" by reasoning that I was drugged for my muscle spasms and still relearning to write. I vowed to never take another psychology class.

Since I was considering majoring in biology or chemistry, I signed up for a chemistry lab. Because I didn't have the physical ability to safely handle chemicals and test tubes, the Disability Resource Center on campus arranged for someone to assist me.

On the first day of class, I was glad to find out "my hands" belonged to a chemistry graduate student. With Bunsen burners glowing and glass flasks and test tubes filled with chemicals, it was great to know he knew what he was doing.

I looked in my lab manual. "Step one is . . ."

Through a thick Indian accent, he said, "I've already completed step one."

"Excuse me?" I asked.

He continued to silently work on the assignment without my input. I felt completely ignored as he worked; I wanted to go step-by-step through the directions so I would understand the chemical reactions.

I looked around the lab. In the station next to me, the

student's liquid concoction didn't look like mine. "What step are you on?"

"Step three," the student responded. He appeared a little irritated at the interruption.

"Which step are you on now?" I asked "my hands" while scanning the lab manual to figure out what was going on.

"Step six."

I let out an exasperated sigh.

Lab after lab followed the same pattern, leaving me stressed and without the knowledge I sought. After that semester, I decided not to take another lab, which ruled out majoring in biology or chemistry.

I look back now and wonder why I gave up so easily.

Diligently studying at my desk in the big family room built after my injury, night after night I sipped Diet Coke and nibbled on peanuts, raisins, and plain M&Ms. Through head-phones, I listened to classical music in an attempt to drown out the clamor of *Wheel of Fortune* and *Jeopardy* flowing through the thin doors that separated me from my parents.

One night, I spent an hour rewriting my messy notes into neat, organized masterpieces. I outlined a chapter from the history textbook so I wouldn't miss a single detail for an upcoming test. I briefly studied for the next day's Spanish quiz, memorizing each of the ten verbs in the subjunctive tense. Trying to get one more thing done, I pushed my chair over to a long table where I had arranged handwritten notecards for a research paper in a religious studies course due in three weeks. I'd soon need to start the slow process of typing the paper, letter by letter, with a pencil I held with a splint.

Make sure to save it to the floppy drive so you don't lose it like you did last time, I chided myself.

"Jen, it's time for bed," Mom called out.

"Ugh. It's already eight thirty?" I moaned.

In addition to a full load of classes, I was living on someone else's schedule for bedtime. On the three nights of the week I did the bowel program, I started getting ready for bed before nine o'clock. Other nights, I was lucky if I studied past nine thirty, but I still needed help from my mom, dad, or grandma to help me transfer into bed, position my body, and pull up the blankets.

The time management skills I honed in gymnastics helped me balance the heavy workload within the confines of a limited schedule without pulling all-nighters like many college students, but I still needed to work hard to earn my above-average grades. My identity was no longer attached to my athletic ability. Instead, I defined myself as a student—a *good* student. I proved my worth, if only to myself, through each A earned.

In my third year of college, my grandma began driving me to school since my friends were no longer attending UofL. By then, she was in her late sixties, with short salt-and-pepper hair, which she set in 1930s-style finger waves with metal clips each morning. The two of us would eat lunch at the Student Activities Center a few days a week. I never felt embarrassed about eating lunch with my grandma in front of other college students. On some level, I understood that most grandmas wouldn't have been able or willing to give up their retirement to help a granddaughter.

On the days I finished classes before lunch, we would meet at the van. Grandma would open the doors, lower the lift, raise it with me on it, and finally latch my manual chair into place by its rear wheels. After arriving home, she'd make a quick lunch for both of us, and we'd settle in the family room and watch a rerun of *Matlock; Murder, She Wrote;* or *Highway to Heaven.*

My grandma was known for having a lead foot. On our way home one day, the van lurched forward a little more quickly than expected, causing me and my chair to flip backward onto the floor. I seemed okay other than the back of my head aching from hitting the carpeted floor. My grandma was oblivious. I yelled, "Um, Grandma, I need some help!"

As she peered into the rearview mirror, she let out a hoot and cried, "Heavens to Betsy!"

All she saw in the mirror were my two feet up in the air where my head should have been. She quickly pulled over to the side of the street. Laughing as she climbed between the front seats, she made her way to the rear of the van and turned me and the chair upright. We continued laughing the whole way home.

When I think back on all the ways Grandma helped me, I can't imagine where I'd be without her support. This is true for so many of the people whom God has placed in my life over the years, including Leslie.

Leslie and I have different versions of how we met at college. I remember being in biology class when I recognized a girl from middle school. Leslie came up to me after class with a ready smile and a Southern drawl and said, "I don't know if you remember me, but we went to Kammerer together."

Leslie recalls asking me if I needed help while I was struggling to push up a ramp and into a building in the rain.

I gladly accepted her assistance, only for her to push me straight into a doorjamb.

"Oh! Did I hurt you?" she asked.

I laughed, while Leslie stood there appalled until she heard my lighthearted reaction to her poor driving skills. "I don't know . . . I can't feel it!"

After taking notes during an hour-long lecture later that semester, I placed my pen on the notebook resting on my lap and slowly moved, stretching my tired and stiff arms and rolling my neck a bit after class had finished. My body rebelled against the slight movement with muscle spasms so violent that my right leg shot out straight, and I kicked the shoe right off my foot clear to the front of the classroom.

"Not again," I said quietly to myself.

Leslie ran and got my shoe.

"You must not like your shoe very much," she joked when she came back. She eased my embarrassment with her sense of humor. "Can I help?"

"If you don't mind," I said.

Leslie knelt in front of me and gently replaced the shoe on the offending foot. At that moment, I knew I had found a friend.

Leslie and I often had lunch together after that, accompanied by my grandma. Between the two of them, their laughter would turn heads.

When we reconnected, I discovered Leslie volunteered as a Young Life leader. I had grown up doing Young Life, a nondenominational Christian outreach for teens, and was excited when she invited me to join them. I showed up the next week and spent the next several years as a Young Life leader. With the meetings, called "club," on one weeknight and leadership meetings at Bill and Hillary McGee's house on Friday evenings, I had a group of peers again and was involved in an activity that was fun and purposeful. The opportunity to pour my time and energy into students' lives was satisfying. My family's world often revolved around me, so it was nice to have the chance to *give* support instead of being the one receiving it.

Leslie has provided more amusement in my life than just about anyone. She has the tendency to get me into sticky situations, then laugh her way out of them. Among our escapades was Leslie's brilliant idea of getting a group together for a city-wide scavenger hunt for Halloween. "There's going to be a bunch of cute guys there," she promised.

The evening started with clues that had us driving all over town: down Lover's Lane (yes, a real road in Louisville), to a creepy old cemetery in Long Run Park, beside the rickety railroad trestle off Taylorsville Road, finally ending up at an old restaurant by a popular movie theater.

To her credit, Leslie called ahead to ask if the haunted house where the event concluded was accessible. They said yes, but I was hesitant. I'd been told too many times that a place was accessible only to find it was not. Despite my misgivings, I got in the long line with Leslie, Jackie, and "the cute guys," after succumbing to peer pressure.

As I rolled into the haunted house, I was blinded by the darkness, followed by flashes of light, and overwhelmed by the loud noises. I maneuvered my power wheelchair, which I often used at this time, moving cautiously through the maze of narrow corridors as chainsaw-wielding murderers, zombies, and vampires jumped out and clawed at us.

My chair suddenly came to a stop. I was caught on something.

"Leslie, I can't move," I yelled over my shoulder. "I think the pin to my tie-down system is caught on something."

Leslie knelt in the tight passageway and saw the metal bolt that locked my chair into my van wedged on the rough flooring.

She shouted over the noise, "Yeah, it's caught."

I backed up in the darkness trying to free myself and felt my chair hit something. Behind me, my friends watched the surprised faces of ghostly actors as a wall came crashing down. Deafened by the loud organ music and spooky sound effects, I had no idea what was going on. I focused on getting through the claustrophobic chaos as quickly as possible, while Leslie shrieked with laughter.

Thankfully, I got my chair over whatever it was stuck on just as two security guards found their way to me in all of the commotion.

"Follow us. We'll show you how to get out."

I slowly moved forward, watching the floor in front of me carefully for more obstacles. At the exit, I saw the "ramp." It was just a flimsy plywood board placed over four or five steps, creating a slope too steep for me to descend safely.

"I can't go down that. Is there another way out?"

Looking back, I saw a line of people waiting for me to move.

"We can pick up your chair," one of the men said.

Frustrated and embarrassed, I realized I had only one choice. "Just make sure to keep the front wheels tilted higher than the back as we go." The last thing I wanted was to be dumped out of my chair.

Behind me, Leslie yelled, "It's really heavy! Don't drop her!"

As I made my way out the exit into the cool and quiet October night, I breathed a sigh of relief. Or exasperation.

I didn't say a word as I smiled, but my eyes must have said it all.

"Jen, I'm so sorry! They said it was accessible," Leslie said, still chuckling.

It's a good thing I really liked her. Even better that she's been a close friend all these years.

However, hidden beneath the laughter I shared with my grandma and Leslie flowed a deep well of inadequacy and shame stemming from my injury. As Proverbs 14:13 (NLT) says, "Laughter can conceal a heavy heart, but when the laughter ends, the grief remains."

And a little side note: it took Leslie twenty-five years to tell me about the wall falling down.

CHAPTER EIGHT

On January 2, 1991—eighteen months after becoming a quadriplegic and just a few weeks shy of my eighteenth birthday—I sat alone in my bedroom with my door closed, feeling a bit melancholy at the beginning of a new year. What was there to celebrate? I felt caged. I dreamt of the independence I once had. I wanted to return to a time when life was easier. Freer.

I opened the top drawer of my dresser and reached to the back where I hid a private journal. At least I hoped it was private. It seemed like anything I thought or did was known by everyone—or at least someone. Privacy was a luxury I no longer had.

Using my stronger left hand, I loosely grasped the small journal, covered in blue material with small white sheep. I flipped it open with my thumb to the inside cover:

Jenny Smith
Given by Barbara for B-day '89
16 yrs. Old

I used to sit on my waterbed late at night in boxer shorts and a T-shirt and record the secrets of my heart. The hand-writing was crisp and angled in the four entries. Blue ink recorded events from a previous life. The journal abruptly ended when my life was interrupted.

I read the first entry about spring break in Destin, Florida, with friends from school—Barbara, Amy, and Heather—at the Roberts' condo on the beach; the condo where my parents were staying when my injury happened. I read how we met a group of boys from Little Rock. We played beach volleyball and sat in the sand listening to one of the guys sing in Spanish. We flirted and enjoyed receiving the attention of a group of boys, some-thing we weren't used to. When we returned to the condo to check in with our moms, the boys serenaded us with "You've Lost That Loving Feeling" while we stood on the balcony. We swooned. If you don't understand the significance of this moment, you're not a child of the '80s. Go watch the movie *Top Gun*.

That was the last time I'd ever feel soft, warm sand between my toes.

I sighed.

I read about my first date, just one month before my injury. I smiled as I was reminded of every detail of riding in his car, going out to eat, and seeing *Indiana Jones and the Last Crusade*.

The third entry was written with exhilaration as I chronicled the phone call I received and how I went to see the new *Batman* movie with him. How I felt awkward around his friends. In the fourth entry, I described scrambling to find a friend so I could watch a movie at his house. I was angry at my mom for not letting me go by myself. (Good job, Mom!)

I picked up my pen, attached to a new, smaller assistive device that slipped onto my pointer finger. I needed to tell the rest of the story. As I balanced the notebook on my lap, I recorded in legible but scrawling handwriting:

We went out a few more times before the accident. He'd come up to the hospital and even brought a movie twice. Eventually, he didn't come to see me anymore.

What more was there to say? I was unwanted. Undesirable. Broken.

I closed the journal and returned it to its hiding place.

During my first summer break from college, my family and I flew to visit my aunts, uncles, and cousins on my mom's side, whom we hadn't seen in years. It was my first experience flying since my accident. The flight was so uneventful I don't remember it.

On a hot afternoon in the suburbs of Phoenix, I watched my brother and two cousins splash in the pool under the blazing sun while I sat in the shade on the patio.

"Jenny, why don't you get in the pool? It's so much cooler in the water," they called out.

"I don't have a swimsuit," I said, trying to find an excuse. I hadn't been swimming since my injury, and I was a bit scared to get into the water.

"You can wear some of my shorts," my cousin Erin offered.

Biting my lip in contemplation, I turned to my mom who was having a conversation with my aunt.

"Mom, could you help me change clothes?" I interrupted. I hated to ask since it was so much work. But it might be fun.

In the guestroom, she helped me transfer to the bed, and we

began the process of taking off my pants and putting on a light pair of workout shorts. Sliding back over the transfer board into my chair proved a bit difficult on bare legs, as my skin didn't smoothly slide over the plastic.

Back outside, I saw my bright white legs glaring in the sun; they were skinny and atrophied, while my feet were slightly swollen and purple from poor circulation. My hands were still lifeless, and although my shoulders were muscular, my forearms were bony and angular where the muscles had wasted away. The borrowed tank top couldn't hide the bane of my existence, my quad belly—the protrusion of my lower abdomen caused by my lack of abdominal muscles. My intestines and other organs pooched out, making my stomach appear like an old man's beer belly.

Sitting in the dry Arizona heat, a slight breeze brushing against my bare shoulders, I recalled what my body looked like two years earlier. My legs were athletic and powerful, but I believed my butt was too big. I thought I was fat. When I went swimming or to the beach during spring break, I'd always worn a T-shirt over my bathing suit or wrapped a towel around myself.

When I quit gymnastics, as I gained a few pounds and my body matured, my body image took a beating. What my body looked like and how much I weighed controlled me. Confined me. The day before my injury I had weighed myself and was so pleased with the number on the scale that I confidently walked out to the pool, not hiding my still-growing five-foot, seven-inch body on that night Barbara and I discussed what it would be like to be paralyzed.

I don't know how or why, but I never struggled with the need to control my weight after my injury. Maybe it was because I was sitting on my "fat butt" and no one could see it or because I had no way to judge myself based on a number on a scale. Maybe it was because I couldn't reach food in the cabinets, open packages containing snacks, or prepare a meal. Or maybe God simply knew I had enough to deal with and graciously removed the struggle to lighten my load.

But the changes to my body after my injury only rubbed salt in an old wound.

Sitting in the sun that afternoon, I had a sudden realization. *You know what, I'm always going to dislike something about my body!*

In that moment, I discovered that whether I thought my butt was too big or my legs too skinny, I was always going to find fault with my body, and somehow the awareness of that fact was freeing. I took a deep breath of the parched desert air like a captive being released.

Matthew and my cousin Adam got out of the pool, splashing water with each footstep and smelling of chlorine. Cold water dripped on me as they picked me up and carried me down the steps into the pool; it wasn't until the water reached my shoulders that I felt the coolness flow over me. Matthew, Adam, and Erin spent the next hour helping me learn how to float and take a few backstrokes in the water using only my arms and head.

I didn't fall in love with my quad belly or my purple feet and swollen ankles that day. But I was beginning to accept that my body—as well as my injury—was a part of me that I could not change.

Back on campus after summer break, I repeatedly passed a girl a few years older than me who also used a wheelchair. I noticed her because she always looked . . . confident. She dressed fashionably, often wearing a miniskirt, and had an air of self-assurance that I lacked. I wanted to know her secret.

The following semester, I saw her as I went from one building to another where my next class was located. I decided to go for it. I pushed toward her.

"Hi. My name is Jenny. And . . . well, you always look so nice!"

Oh, my gosh! What did I just say? I felt my cheeks grow warm with embarrassment.

"Um, thanks. I'm Terri," she said tentatively.

Words rushed from my mouth. "I don't know anyone else who uses a wheelchair. I'm still new to this. My injury was about two years ago."

"I was in a car accident when I was seventeen. It's been seven years for me," Terri explained. "I'm going to class in Davidson Hall. Where's your next class?"

"I'm going to Davidson too."

We both started pushing in the direction of our classes. Terri easily pushed up the ramp to the building. I could tell she had a low-level spinal cord injury; she had full use of her hands and arms and leaned forward as she pushed up the ramp without losing her balance. She made it look easy.

If only I could use my hands.

Push by push, I slowly made my way up the long ramp. I finally caught up with her at the top of the incline.

"I've got to get to class, but it was nice meeting you," I said.

"You too. I'll see you around."

Terri was the first woman my age using a wheelchair who I truly got to know. Until I met Terri, I was convinced that I wasn't "one of them." You know, someone with a disability. Yes, I had a spinal cord injury, but I wasn't "disabled." I held stereotypes and prejudices about people with disabilities, even if I didn't realize it.

After a few months of chatting between classes, Terri invited me to her home, a brick ranch-style house with a steep ramp leading up to the front door. Although the inside of the house wasn't converted to be accessible like mine, she had modified how she did things, such as using a spatula to reach a cup in the kitchen cabinets above her countertop. She made it work.

Terri lived alone, had a boyfriend, and worked a part-time job in addition to going to college. Over time, she had adapted to life with a wheelchair. Terri showed me that living with a disability didn't have to define or limit who I was or what I was capable of doing.

Terri was living a life I didn't know was possible as a wheelchair user.

Finally accepting the reality of my new life allowed me to see the potential of a world of opportunities. I couldn't begin to imagine what my life would look like, but if Terri could do it, I might just be able to do it as well.

CHAPTER NINE

S itting in a sterile white room at the doctor's office, I nervously rehearsed what I wanted to ask.

For several years I had held out hope that I'd be in the one percent who would overcome the odds. I continued to go to PT a few times a week. Although I was stronger, I still couldn't use my hands. I had hoped God would heal me, as so many people had prayed—and continued to pray. But by the third year after my accident, I was accepting the permanence of my spinal cord injury. If my injury was "forever," then I needed to do something about my muscle spasms.

Although I was taking four oral medications to control them, the spasms were so severe that my legs would extend out straight or pull in so forcefully that the Velcro strap behind my legs on the footrest would break. My upper body would be pulled forward, then tossed backward and sideways when my abdominal and back muscles contracted. My fingers balled up in fists so tight that my nails would leave impressions in the palms of my hands. At the same time, the medicine made my eyes so heavy I often dozed off in class.

The click-clack of my doctor's high heels approaching the door brought me back to the present. Dr. Gleis, with her bright blue eyes, dark hair, and red lips, always reminded me of Lynda Carter from TV's *Wonder Woman*.

After a few greetings, I got to the point.

"My spasms are so bad I'm willing to do anything. I've heard about something called an alcohol wash. It kills the nerves. Would this help?"

I knew the procedure would destroy any chance I had of walking again.

After thinking for a moment, Dr. Gleis responded, "There might be a better option. A research study is about to begin where a pump is implanted into the abdomen. It's about the size of a hockey puck. A small tube runs from the pump into the spinal fluid that surrounds the spinal cord. The medicine is delivered directly where it's needed to relax the spasms. I think you should speak to Dr. Watkins about the study."

Several weeks later, I lay in a hospital bed as a doctor gave me a test dose of baclofen through a spinal tap. About an hour after the medication had been injected into my spinal fluid, he moved each leg through a series of range-of-motion exercises. My legs were flaccid and could be moved without resistance. For the first time in three years, my body wasn't hijacked by spasms. It was a miracle.

With little hesitation and much hope, I underwent surgery with Dr. Nazar, the same neurosurgeon who performed my spinal fusion. For three long days after surgery, I had to lie flat on my back to allow the surgical site to heal and to minimize the excruciating spinal headache caused by the loss of spinal fluid during the operation.

After the surgery, the spasticity no longer controlled my life. I reduced and eventually eliminated the oral medications.

I was free from the prison of spasticity.

~

Soon after receiving the pump, I experienced another freedom.

I sat in my power wheelchair and watched a ramp fold out of the passenger-side sliding door of a gray 1992 Plymouth Voyager. I could hardly believe this was *my* van that *I* would drive! With the money raised after my injury, we'd purchased the minivan, and Kentucky's Office of Vocational Rehabilitation paid for the modifications. I rolled up the ramp and positioned my chair in front of the steering wheel. The chair clicked into a lock on the floor of the van, holding it securely in place.

Clinton Matney, the driving instructor provided by the state, sat in the passenger seat, his gravelly voice explaining how I would drive with hand controls. "We've installed a temporary brake on the passenger side, just in case you decide to try something crazy."

I looked over and saw his right foot near a brake.

"Turn on the engine," he instructed.

With the back of my hand, I pulled up on the metal extension we added to the key to make turning it easier. The engine roared to life.

"Now place your left hand in the tri-pin."

I slipped my left hand into a three-pronged brace called a tri-pin; two prongs snugly held my wrist in place, and a third extension supported my hand and fingers.

"While the van is in park, I want you to pull gently back on the gas to get a feel for it."

With some hesitation, I pulled back on the gas and heard the engine hum.

"Now push forward to apply the brakes."

As I pushed forward on the hand controls, I saw the foot pedal for the brake move down toward the floor.

"Tip the hand control side to side to turn on the blinkers."

I tilted the tri-pin to the left, heard the rhythmic sound of the blinker, and saw the dashboard light up with the turn indicator. I tipped it to the left again, and it turned off.

"Good. Now put your right hand in the tri-pin on the steering wheel."

The second tri-pin sat at the five o'clock position on the steering wheel. I slipped my hand into it and easily turned the steering wheel, first one full rotation to the right, then a full spin to the left. The modified zero-effort steering was easier to turn than standard power steering.

"What's this?" I asked, looking down at a circular four-inch-wide red button fastened to the driver's door.

"That's how you control the wipers, bright lights, and horn."

I tapped the red button with my elbow, and the wipers came on. Another tap turned them off. I smiled and giggled with delight.

"All right, ready to give this a try?"

I took a deep breath and nodded, following his step-by-step instructions.

"Push forward on the brake. Take your hand out of the steering wheel and put the van in drive. There you go. Put your hand back in the tri-pin. And now let's gently pull back on the brake."

Out of the corner of my eye, I saw Clinton's foot slide closer to the passenger brake. I pulled back on the gas, and the van jumped forward more quickly than I expected.

"That's touchy!" I exclaimed, quickly letting off the gas and applying the brake. I tried again, lightly pulling back on the control, and the van moved forward smoothly.

I spent the next five days driving several hours a day with Clinton. We started on roads with little traffic, eventually building up to driving on busier roads. Finally, I got on the interstate. After a week, I was handed the keys and officially cleared to drive.

I was free!

Clinton was the first person to recommend that I use a power chair full-time so I would be completely independent on ramps or rough terrain. My new van had a steep ramp, and I couldn't push up it by myself. Without a power chair, I'd need to have help whenever I wanted to drive.

I wasn't very happy about primarily using a power chair since I felt more disabled in it, even though it gave me more independence. There's an unspoken hierarchy among wheel-chair users: those who use manual chairs are tougher, stronger, and less impaired, while power chair users are idle, weak, and more physically impaired. It's unfair—and untrue—but exists among my circle of friends.

With the power chair, I was completely independent from dawn till dusk with little impact on my energy level. If I were going somewhere I knew was inaccessible, such as a friend's house or restaurant, I'd bring my manual chair and transfer into it and be lifted into the house. A power chair weighs hundreds of pounds, while a manual chair is typically less than twenty pounds. To stay in shape, I pushed around the neighborhood in my manual chair or used it on days when I didn't leave the house.

Eating some humble pie, I have to admit Clinton made the right suggestion about the power chair. I can't help but make the comparison to my spiritual life. I frequently try to do things with my own strength. More often than not, I end up frustrated and exhausted, just as if I'm pushing up a steep ramp in my manual chair. Ephesians 3:20 (NLT) says, "All glory to God, who is able, through his mighty power at work within us, to accomplish infinitely more than we ask or think." Whether it's using a power chair to give me a boost up a ramp or asking God for strength to endure the hardships in life, sometimes I need to accept the help that's available so I can accomplish more than is possible in my limited strength.

Another benefit of the power chair: I haven't suffered from overuse of my shoulders, which frequently happens for long-term manual chair users. As Dr. Watkins once told me, "Your shoulders weren't made for walking."

CHAPTER TEN

The year I began driving again, I also had my first summer job working as a customer service representative for Sears Teleservice. I sat in a small cubicle with a device on my left hand to type and a similar device on my right hand which held a pen. I took notes as I spoke with customers who needed to schedule repairs on their appliances. I quickly discovered that talking with disgruntled customers was not my forte. I gladly returned to classes when the semester began.

The following summer, I worked at the YMCA's Childcare Enrichment Program. After several years of teaching Sunday school to kindergartners, I thought it might be a better fit. I was assigned to a group of kindergartners and relished my time as they colored and played board games, tromped around the playground, and asked such honest questions, none of which seemed off limits. I loved their honesty, with one exception when a six-year-old asked as she pointed to my quad belly, "Is there a baby in your tummy, Miss Jenny?"

One sunny day we were out on the playground. The kids

were hanging on monkey bars and playing tag in the mulched area around the swings.

"Red group, line up, please! It's time to go inside," I announced as loudly as I could. Once I had my gaggle together, the children started walking toward the school.

"Hey, guys, hold on a second," I pushed my joystick forward, but my power chair wouldn't move. I checked the gears and the lights on the battery meter. With a sinking feeling, I saw the battery light wasn't even lit. It had completely died.

Do I send one kid in to get an adult or send all of them in? This wasn't something they covered in training.

"Collin, will you go find Mr. Todd and ask him to come outside, please?"

Soon Todd walked outside looking a bit confused.

"My chair has died. I'm going to need a push to my van and to go home," I said apologetically.

I explained to Todd how to manually switch gears on the chair so he could push me to the parking lot. Curious five- and six-years-olds watched as I opened my magic van and was pushed up the ramp. When I started driving, my parents had insisted on a hardwired car phone for situations like this. When I got home, I called and asked to be rescued from my van.

I look back on that day and am grateful none of the kids ran into the street or got in a fight while I was a sitting duck, unable to move. By working part-time jobs, I learned valuable lessons, including my likes and dislikes for future career opportunities.

Entering my fourth year at the University of Louisville, I still was clueless when it came to choosing a major. My "problem" was that I liked all the classes I took, whether they were in science, math, Spanish, history, or religious studies. Wanting to graduate, I made an appointment with the advising office to seek help in choosing a major. The office was in a building called Gardiner Hall, which was built in 1872. I went to the accessible entrance at the back of the building and rang the doorbell. When someone opened the door, I took a tiny elevator to the second floor and arrived for my appointment early, as usual.

"Which major will take all my credits and allow me to graduate the soonest?" I asked.

The advisor grabbed a large book from the bookcase behind her. After reviewing my transcripts, she replied, "Psychology."

I believe I audibly moaned. I had sworn to never take another psychology course. But in my fourth year of college, I started taking several psychology classes each semester so I could graduate. I'll admit I even enjoyed the classes focused on the biological bases of behavior and psychology.

While finishing my final two semesters part-time, I volunteered at the Crisis and Information Center, a suicide and information hotline for the community. I thought it might be useful to get entry-level experience in the field. Through the hotline, I discovered my ability to listen and work well with people experiencing crises.

In May of 1995, I graduated cum laude. It had taken me five years, but I had a bachelor's degree in psychology with a concentration in natural sciences and a minor in religious studies.

Completing college is typically a transition point to adulthood. At least it was in the '90s. Although I had successfully graduated, I didn't feel like an adult who was ready to conquer the world. I was still living at home, and I was dependent on my parents and Grandma for many of my daily needs.

Just before I received my undergraduate degree, I hired a personal care attendant. I didn't want to do it, and I fought the idea when my mom mentioned it. It was horrifying enough to have my mom and Grandma help me with personal care. But a stranger? No way! However, between my mom working full-time and experiencing increasing back problems and Grandma being, well, a grandma, it needed to happen.

Hiring someone to help me every morning was the best thing that could have happened for everyone. Looking back, I wish we would have made the decision sooner. By having a personal care attendant in the mornings, I wasn't cranky and short-tempered with my family, and I felt like less of a burden. With outside help, I was in more control of my schedule and how I wanted things done. Although my mom still helped me three nights a week with the bowel program, I was learning to take control of my care and advocate for my needs.

Driving had given me the ability to attend a new church with a singles class where I had a group of friends my age. I continued to volunteer as a leader with Young Life. Part-time jobs and volunteering at the crisis center helped me discover what I was good at and enjoyed, but I still didn't know what I wanted to do for a career. Since I wasn't quite ready to try "adulting," graduate school seemed to be the easiest next step. However, I experienced a few unexpected pit stops before I would make it into the world of work.

CHAPTER ELEVEN

The summer after I graduated from college, my brother invited me to go to a water park to spend time with his girlfriend whom he had met on a skiing trip with mutual friends. Misty had dark hair and hazel-green eyes, and was double majoring in psychology and sociology at Western Kentucky University. It was easy to see why Matthew had fallen for her. The cool water felt great during the heat and humidity of a Kentucky summer as the three of us were riding the waves and chatting in the wave pool.

After a half an hour, my arms were cramping from holding on to the inflatable raft.

"I think I need to rest a bit. Could you help me out?"

Matthew picked me up and carried me out of the pool and set me down near the water's edge. After catching my breath, I realized the "beach" was concrete and I should probably sit on my cushion.

"Matthew, could you grab the cushion off my chair for me?" He ran over and grabbed it, and as I lifted my body with my arms, he slid the cushion under my bottom.

People with spinal cord injuries have to be aware of skin breakdown, which can occur on their bottom, heels, elbows, and other bony places. Without sensation, we can't feel pain or the tingling sensation someone gets that signals blood circulation has been impaired, such as when an arm or leg goes to sleep. What happens when you've been sitting in an uncomfortable chair and your butt starts to hurt? You feel it, or at least your brain registers there's a problem, and you change positions. Individuals with spinal cord injuries lack that feedback from our bodies, so we use specialized cushions and practice "pressure relief"—changing our position to keep the blood flowing— every thirty minutes to ensure the skin doesn't get damaged.

Those sixty seconds without a cushion were one of the worst mistakes of my life. Sitting on the concrete with wet, delicate skin, along with the back-and-forth shearing motion caused by the waves was a trifecta for disaster.

A few days later while my mom was helping me undress, she said, "You have a spot on your butt bone. I've never seen it red like this before."

I wasn't able to do my personal care at the time, so when my mom mentioned the redness on my left butt bone, it was out of sight and out of mind. I remembered learning something in rehab about staying off your bottom if it was red, but surely it wasn't that bad.

"I've got to go to school. I can't stay off my bottom," I told her. My first semester of graduate school seemed more important than a small red spot I couldn't see or feel.

That fall I'd started classes for my master's degree in counseling psychology. I never wanted an undergraduate degree in psychology, much less a graduate degree. Whenever someone asks why I got my master's in counseling psychology, I simply say, "God made me do it." As Proverbs 3:5-6 (NLT) says, "Trust in the Lord with all your heart; do not depend on your own understanding. Seek his will in all you do, and he will show you which path to take." In my gut, I knew this program was the next right step.

I never saw the red spot that quickly developed into a nickel-sized open pressure sore, exposing layers of fat and muscle tissue. At the time, there were no cell phones to snap a picture so I could see the damage. I ignored my mom's concerns and continued attending classes and studying.

Finally, at my mom's insistence, I went to see Dr. Watkins.

"Jenny, this is a Stage 4 wound. It's down to the bone. You've got to stay off it and see a plastic surgeon." The concern in his voice told me I needed to obey his instructions.

A pressure sore develops from reduced blood flow to the skin, from shearing, or from deep tissue damage after a missed transfer or fall. Since they often develop from the inside out, by the time my mom saw an open wound, it was really too late. If I would have stayed off my bottom when she first told me the area was red, it would have healed in a few weeks, and I wouldn't have needed three surgeries over the next four years.

Pressure sores are not just an inconvenience; they can be deadly. Actor Christopher Reeve, despite his Superman persona, died from complications of a pressure sore. If it doesn't kill you, it sure makes life miserable, requiring weeks, months, or even years in bed.

My first surgery was during Christmas break. The procedure is called a skin flap. Dr. Derr cut away dead skin and muscle and pulled and sewed together the healthy tissue. Since I'm quite bony, he also chipped the ischial bone down. I not-so-jokingly suggested breast implants in my butt. He didn't find that amusing.

Healing from a skin flap takes time. I lay in bed four weeks.

No. Getting. Up. At the end of week four, an ambulance took me to Dr. Derr's office, where he examined me and said I was allowed to get up for thirty minutes four times a day, for a total of two hours, during the next week. After one week, I was able to start sitting up for an hour four times a day. Once my skin tolerated sitting up two hours at a time four times a day during the third week, I was given the okay to sit up full-time, as long as I did proper pressure relief by lifting my body with my arms or shifting my weight every thirty minutes.

For the first half of my spring semester of grad school, I was in bed. I'd lie on my stomach, propped on my elbows, with my head at the foot of the bed where a piano bench held my books. My elbows became bloodied from supporting my upper body for so long. I was back at school by the end of the spring semester. I had learned my lesson the hard way. At least I thought I had.

During my second year of graduate school, I applied for a part-time position as a teaching assistant at Norton Elementary School, the school I had attended in fifth grade and where my mom still worked. I worked nine hours a week, which was plenty since I was in school full-time.

I worked one-on-one with several students who were considered "at risk" educationally and socially. In a small room off the library, I spent about an hour with each student, listening to them, getting to know them, laughing at their stories, and, of course, tutoring. One girl had recently emigrated from a country in Africa and was behind in her education and didn't speak much English. She timidly smiled as she read new words and when we carried on brief conversations.

Another student, Jonathan, was considered a trouble-maker. In third grade, he was short and stocky and had dreams of becoming a University of Louisville basketball player. I may have covertly suggested playing football instead. Jonathan knew how to push the teacher's buttons, but I always looked forward to my time with him. I often had to suppress laughter when he joked around or talked in circles to avoid doing his work. He could use his brain when he was encouraged to do so, and I saw potential in him.

For the first time since I coached gymnastics, I felt something click. I was born to do this. I wasn't sure what "this" was yet, but I realized that coaching gymnastics and tutoring required the ability to teach, encourage, and practice patience.

I was finding the gifts and talents I used in tutoring brought me joy. I didn't need to rely on my identity as a gymnast or good student to "be someone." It was an important step in discovering who I was and what I was capable of accomplishing.

When I was halfway through my internship for assessing clients using psychological tests and exams, I sat in a large meeting room at a table and my supervisor—an experienced, silver-haired psychologist—stood imposingly in front of me. He handed me my evaluation form. I looked through the feedback to make sure all of the "above average" and "excellent" options were circled. When my eyes saw "average" or "needs improvement" circled, my stomach dropped. I kept my gaze on the piece of paper, unable to look at him.

After a few moments, he broke the awkward silence. "You can improve in those areas," he said bluntly.

I felt like I was back in middle school, standing in front of my coach while he criticized me. Except I couldn't pretend to not hear it. Tears trickled from my eyes, only increasing my shame.

As I wiped a tear away, he quickly said, "*That*! That's what I want to see more of."

I raised my eyes to meet his, furrowing my eyebrows in confusion, as he leaned over the table, crossed out "needs improvement," and circled "average."

"I want to see more of *you*. What's inside that head of yours?"

I didn't have an answer for him. I decided it was time to find some help in figuring that out.

During my sophomore year of college, a friend from school, Natalie, made me see a counselor as a condition of driving me to social activities. With my freedom on the line, I grudgingly accepted the terms of her blackmail.

I'm not sure what had happened to make Natalie think I needed to see a counselor. I know I was . . . um, *am* . . . quite grumpy when I have to rely on others. I remember being irritable and blaming a friend who didn't tell me I'd had a bladder accident, even though she wasn't at fault. I was constantly short-tempered with my parents. Natalie had seen a counselor after the death of a family member and decided it would be helpful for me too.

After my injury, my mom became depressed and saw a counselor. I've noticed it's the moms who often have a more difficult time coping with a child's injury than the child does. For one of my mom's sessions, Tacie, her counselor, requested the family attend. The first time I met Tacie was at her house. She was lying on a long stretcher with large wheels that she pushed with her arms while healing from a pressure sore. She, too, had a spinal cord injury.

When my friend insisted I see a counselor, Tacie was the only one I knew. Natalie drove me to Tacie's house where we'd agreed to meet. I pushed up the front ramp, and she answered the door, now sitting in her manual chair. She showed me around her kitchen, bedroom, and bathroom. Her house was set up perfectly for her needs as a paraplegic who had full use of her hands and arms.

As I think back, Tacie served more as a mentor than a counselor. She told me about her history of depression, which was indirectly the cause of her injury when she attempted suicide during a manic phase of bipolar disorder. She talked to me about her feelings of loss, how she had successfully raised her girls by herself, and how the most satisfying romantic relationship of her life was after her injury. I have a feeling she did more talking than I did, but her example was what I needed. And I think she sensed I wasn't ready to go much further at that point.

My professors in the master's program encouraged students to experience therapy for themselves. I still didn't want to, although I had begun to see the need. This time, a friend didn't make me pick up the phone and schedule an appointment.

I looked for a counselor who wouldn't know me or my story. I was paranoid about someone "finding out," despite the fact I was going to school to be a counselor. Unfortunately, seeking therapy is still stigmatized, and I was afraid of someone judging me. With a pounding heart, behind the closed door of my bedroom, I picked up the phone, pushed each number with the knuckle of my pinky finger, and made an appointment.

"What brings you in?" the receptionist asked over the phone.

"I have to see a counselor as a requirement for school" was the best reply I could come up with. It was a half-truth.

For the next several months, I'd leave the house telling my

parents I had a meeting for school. They never questioned me, but I'm sure they had to know something was up.

The counselor was good at guiding me through talking about family issues and the losses related to my injury. I spoke of the shame I carried for needing help with dressing and my bowel program. She invited me to participate in group therapy where I could practice accepting as well as giving feedback.

It was one small step, but at least I was on my way. One thing I do know is God stretched me emotionally because I was willing to do something that didn't make sense to me. I can say with confidence that if the emotional growth I experienced was all I acquired from graduate school, it was worth it.

What I didn't know was I would eventually use everything I learned during those three years in ways I never imagined.

CHAPTER TWELVE

Terri, my friend from the University of Louisville, entered the Ms. Wheelchair America pageant and won the 1998 national title. In her new role, she was responsible for starting a state pageant in Kentucky. She'd been an independent delegate in the national pageant since Kentucky didn't have a state competition.

"I think you should enter Ms. Wheelchair Kentucky, Jenny," Terri said. "We still need a few contestants."

"Uh . . . I don't think so." A competition where I'd have to speak in front of groups as a representative for the disabled community? "No way."

"I think you would do a great job. I had so much fun at the national pageant. Think about it at least?"

Hearing the excitement in Terri's voice had piqued my curiosity. I thought about it. I had been speaking to schools and churches over the past several years, telling my story and educating others about spinal cord injuries. With Terri's positive peer pressure, I reluctantly agreed to enter the pageant. Little did I know how Terri's encouragement to get outside my comfort zone would change the way I viewed myself and my disability.

The Ms. Wheelchair America program is not a beauty pageant; its focus is on advocacy and educating the public on behalf of the millions of people with disabilities in the United States. Contestants are judged on their communication skills, advocacy efforts, and achievements. Thank heavens, there is no bathing suit competition!

Kentucky's first pageant, in May 1998, was a small event where the three judges outnumbered the two contestants: Robin and me. After a morning of closed judging sessions where we answered questions in front of the panel of judges, I dressed for the main event. In a private room at the United Way building in downtown Louisville, my mom helped me change from business attire to a floor-length black sleeveless dress with a crocheted black cardigan. A strand of my mom's pearls and dangly pearl earrings were my only adornments. I added red lipstick for a pop of color. The stylish bob I now had—with a fringe of straight-cut bangs—was a huge improvement over the permed hair I'd had for the first several years of college.

"Go break a leg!" my mom encouraged as she double-checked that my dress was draped over my legs and feet.

I rolled my eyes and chuckled nervously.

Robin and I waited outside the conference hall where the pageant was held. Hearing the music begin was our cue to make an entrance. Escorted by her husband, Robin wore a long white skirt and blazer as she rolled down the center aisle, taking her place on the right, while my dad walked beside me to the left side of the ballroom and we positioned ourselves opposite Robin.

Tom Wills, a meteorologist for a local TV station, was the emcee. As he welcomed everyone, I gazed out at the audience. I made eye contact with my young cousins from St. Louis, sitting next to my mom, grandma, and aunt. I gave them a wink and a smile.

The final judging session arrived, and Tom held several questions in sealed envelopes.

I tried to exhale the nerves out of my body. We were told we'd have one "fun" question and one advocacy-related question. Tom walked toward me, holding two envelopes. I pointed to the envelope on the right. Unsealing the envelope, he looked down and read the question: "If you could choose to be any animal, which would you choose and why?"

I was surprised when an answer quickly came to mind. My dad held the microphone for me as I answered. "I'd be a monkey so I could swing from tree branches just as I did when I was a gymnast."

The crowd politely clapped as I wondered if my response was too corny.

After Robin and I had answered both our questions, the judges left the auditorium to tally their results and make a decision. Ms. Wheelchair Tennessee provided entertainment by singing as we waited.

Finally, the judges returned to the table in front of the stage and handed the results to Tom. I felt my stomach flip-flop with anticipation.

"The first runner-up is . . ." He paused as he opened the envelope and unfolded a piece of paper, "Robin Head."

As the audience applauded, I looked up at my dad in disbelief.

"Ms. Wheelchair Kentucky 1998 is Jenny Smith," Tom announced. The audience cheered and clapped as I maneuvered my power chair to center stage next to Terri, who was wearing the perfect little black dress.

"I told you you'd do great," she whispered as I ducked my head so she could drape the white sash across my body. Then she carefully positioned the tiara on my head.

Tom held the microphone in front of me. "My first official act as Ms. Wheelchair Kentucky is to invite everyone to a reception in the back of the auditorium." The small audience applauded again as the state coordinator walked over and congratulated me.

My cousins, seven and eleven at the time, ran up to congratulate me. My aunt snapped a picture of the three of us. A local news station interviewed me. I was back in the spotlight again, but this time I was more confident and in control.

The next step was raising the money to attend the national pageant in Charlotte, North Carolina. With the support of my friends, family, and community, I raised the money for the registration fee, wardrobe, and airfare. My parents, grandma, and I flew to Charlotte, while extended family drove from Chicago and St. Louis to cheer for me.

The first evening's event was quite a sight: twenty-six women with varying disabilities, ranging in age from twenty-one to sixty-two crowded into a conference room at the hotel. The theme that night was "Let's Make a Deal." I'd never heard of the gameshow, but we were instructed to wear crazy costumes. Leslie Ostrander and her husband, Aaron, were a nerdy couple, complete with pocket protectors, suspenders, and taped eyeglasses. Elaine made a beautiful Cleopatra, and I wore a bright blue Middle Eastern-inspired outfit with dramatic cat-eyed eyeliner.

Conversation came easily and naturally with the other contestants. I quickly connected with Leslie's warm and fun-natured personality. Her strong Georgia accent oozed of Southern charm and pageant life; in fact, I learned she had competed in pageants alongside able-bodied women from her chair. I noticed Leslie had a bit of hand function and the back of her wheelchair sat very low, just above her hips. She didn't even use armrests on her manual chair as I did at the time.

"What level injury do you have?" I asked.

"C7. But I have some grip with my left hand, and I can extend my fingers on the right."

"How were you injured?"

"When I was four years old, I was in a car accident. I was sitting on my grandmother's lap, and there were no seatbelt laws. She was killed but saved my life holding onto me."

"Oh, I'm sorry." I realized everyone here had a story. "Who is here to help you get dressed and . . . with all the other stuff?"

"No one. I'm here with my husband, Aaron. We're newly-weds!" she said blissfully. "I do everything on my own."

Leslie was completely independent and able to dress, shower, and manage her bladder and bowel care. I didn't even know that was possible for a quad. I had so many questions. Thankfully, I had twenty-five women to learn from during the next week.

The next day we all went to Carowinds, a local theme park. Leslie, Kristine, and I explored the amusement park together with Leslie's husband and my parents in tow.

"Let's go on this roller coaster!" cried Leslie.

"Um," I replied hesitantly. "I've not been on a roller coaster since I was injured."

"Oh, it's fun. There's nothing to it. Come on, try it!" Kristine pleaded.

My parents lifted me into the seat of a rickety, wooden roller coaster; my mom sat next to me, and we pulled down the safety bar, which rested several inches above our laps. I held on for dear life with my left arm wrapped around my mom and my right wrist pulled against the safety bar in an attempt to keep my balance. Leslie and Kristine were right: this was fun! However, as the ride came to an end, the brakes brought the cars to an abrupt halt; I couldn't brace my body with my legs, and before I knew it, I slid off the short, slippery seat and under the safety bar.

"Agh!" I exclaimed. "I wasn't expecting that!"

"Are you okay?" my mom asked as she helped me back onto the seat.

"I'm fine, just a little light-headed." I laughed.

Our small group rolled around the park until Leslie and Kristine decided to go on another roller coaster—one that had several upside-down loops and corkscrews.

They started to push toward the accessible entrance for the ride. I didn't move.

I wasn't quite brave enough to try this one and opted out. Sliding off the seat on the last ride seemed like enough excitement for one day. I went to the platform and watched both of them gracefully transfer from their chairs to the floor, then scoot over into the seats. As a quad, Leslie's abilities, fine-tuned from an early age, amazed me. The roller coaster sped off.

Several minutes later, Leslie and Kristine returned with windblown hair and huge smiles. I got bombarded with pleas.

"Jenny, you've got to ride this. You can do it!"

Aaron, Leslie's husband, offered to ride with me.

Gathering my courage, I said, "Okay." *Besides, this roller coaster has a chest harness and goes upside down, so the blood will rush to my head, and my blood pressure won't drop,* I convinced myself, still feeling light-headed from the previous ride.

Aaron lifted me into the seat and strapped my legs together with his belt so they wouldn't flop around. Pulling down the chest harness, I felt safe and secure. I was really going to do this!

As we approached the first loop, the speed pushed me tightly against the back of the seat. Seeing the world from an inverted position was exhilarating; I hadn't been upside down in nine years; it was the closest to gymnastics I could get.

I felt my blood pressure plummet.

"Um, Aaron, I just want to let you know I'm going to pass out," I said as my vision faded and my hearing became muffled. I was unconscious before he responded.

A few seconds later, I came to and said, "I'm back!"

I discovered my blood pressure theory had been flawed; adding g-forces to already low blood pressure isn't a great idea. But I did it.

The pageant began the next day with two days of interview sessions in front of a panel of judges. I answered questions about disability advocacy to the best of my ability. That evening we let loose at a 1970s-themed party. I had never been a dancer, unless a choreographed floor or beam routine counts, but I felt comfortable in my own skin with these women who also used chairs, and I slowly made my way to the dance floor. Shackles of shame and embarrassment that had bound me for years were slowly being removed by the positive and fun-loving nature of these women.

The following evening, we gave a three-minute judged speech explaining our platform. After much thought, as Ms. Wheelchair Kentucky, I'd decided to make my platform for the year educating children about people with disabilities. Through my interaction with kids while teaching and speaking, I discovered that allowing children to ask questions and honestly answering those questions removed the stigma and fear associated with disability.

The fifth and final day was the actual pageant. My mom helped me get into my floor-length, glittery, flesh-toned sleeveless dress that accentuated my broad shoulders. I carefully put on pageant-worthy makeup and berry-colored lipstick. Volunteers styled my hair.

As we waited for the pageant to begin, my mom took a picture of Leslie and me. Leslie was dressed in full pageant attire with dangling earrings and a silver-and-black sequined dress. The anticipation of the beginning of the event had some contestants chatting nervously, while others, like me, sat silently. One by one, we pushed onto the stage with an escort at our side; we stated our name and the state we represented. Then the top ten finalists were announced.

I didn't make the top ten, but that didn't matter. I learned the valuable lesson that when I faced my fears and intentionally got outside of my comfort zone, I experienced opportunities that were life changing. Yes, it had been intimidating, but the payoff was more than worth the temporary discomfort.

I also realized there is strength in numbers. Surrounded by twenty-five women with similar struggles, I witnessed an even bigger world of possibilities than Lois, Terri, and Tacie had exemplified. The contestants had been willing to openly and

honestly answer my questions and show me that living independently—even as a quad—was possible.

But the life I desired still seemed just out of reach. Leslie
had some function in her hands; the ability to grip with one
hand seemed to make a world of difference. What would be
possible if I could use my hands just a little bit?

CHAPTER THIRTEEN

I n December 1998, I graduated with my master's degree in counseling psychology from the University of Louisville. Although I was uncertain of my future career, I was sure of one thing: I was taking a year off from my responsibilities for a series of surgeries.

Nine years after my injury, my mom came home from Bible study and said, "I met Sharon Shaw tonight. Her husband is a surgeon and rehab doctor. She thinks you should talk to him about tendon transfers."

I had heard about the surgery shortly after my injury, but at the time, I wasn't interested. The procedure transfers a functioning muscle and its tendon, such as a wrist muscle, and surgically moves them to allow the transferred muscle to perform a new action, such as forming a grasp with the hand. After my injury, I held out hope that I would regain the use of my hands. And in all honestly, I didn't want to have the large scars that would be visible as a result of each surgery.

But this time, as soon as my mom mentioned the surgery, I knew it was time. I was ready.

Dr. John Shaw is a physical medicine and rehabilitation doctor, as well as an orthopedic surgeon. He and his wife served as medical missionaries in South Korea from 1972 until 1984. It was in Korea, working with polio patients, that Dr. Shaw became adept at performing the intricate procedure.

I scheduled an appointment and met Dr. Shaw in his New Albany, Indiana, office, a thirty-minute drive from where we lived.

Dr. Shaw, with a full head of gray hair and a soft-spoken demeanor explained the complicated surgery of transferring one functioning muscle and tendon to use in another capacity.

"Let me test your wrist strength," he said.

I extended my left arm toward him.

"Resist me as I push down on your hand."

I successfully held up my wrist against the pressure he applied.

"Good. You've got full function on that side. Let's try the right side."

"This one's a lot weaker," I warned.

Dr. Shaw easily pushed it down in spite of my best effort.

"On your left side, we can do a transfer with your middle wrist muscle to give you a good, strong grip. But your right side is too weak. If I did the surgery on your right hand, you might lose much of your wrist function. But I can give you a pinch in both thumbs and a tricep on your right arm."

Although I could pick up items such as a light plastic cup using tenodesis, trying to hold a heavy glass of water at a restaurant could be disastrous. I still used adaptive devices for writing and putting on my makeup. Having a grip with my fingers in my left hand and using my thumb to pick up objects sounded incredible.

"How many surgeries will it take?" I asked.

"Four. We'll spread them out over a year, if you're up for it."

"What about the scars?" I said with apprehension.

"I'll do my best to make sure you can barely see them," he promised.

~

In January 1999, I was on a stretcher in the cold preoperative room, shivering despite the layers of warm blankets piled upon me. An IV was in my left arm. I knew I was in good hands since Dr. Shaw was one of a small group of experienced surgeons who performed this surgery in the United States. But once I was in the pre-op room, all of the certainty I had vanished. *What if this doesn't work? What if something goes wrong?*

As if on cue, Dr. Shaw entered the room and greeted me with his smile. He again reviewed the basics of what he was going to do during the first surgery. Then it was time. Fear bubbled up enough that I had to hold back tears.

"Jenny, can I pray with you before we go into surgery?" he asked.

"Yes," I said gratefully. "Please."

Knowing that I was in expert hands was a comfort. But the greater sense of security came from knowing that Dr. Shaw was not relying solely on his skills as a trained surgeon but on the God who gave him the incredible gift of restoration and healing.

The healing of my hands didn't come in the form I expected or wanted. But God had been working behind the scenes by introducing me to Terri at college, showing me Leslie's level of independence at the Ms. Wheelchair America pageant, and bringing my mom and Sharon together at Bible study at just the right time. In my small group Bible study, I struggled to understand—and believe—how "in all things God works for the good of those who love him" (Rom. 8:28 NIV). I still can't comprehend how God brings good from horrible circumstances, but examples like this one have given me a small glimpse into the bigger picture of seeing God at work in my life.

~

The first tendon transfer was on my right arm. The posterior deltoid, one of three muscles in the shoulder, was anchored to my elbow so I could activate it and use it as a tricep. Since my injury, I hadn't had any use of my right tricep, which enables raising the arm above the head and extending the arm; dressing and transferring are just two of the many ways a tricep is used every day.

When I woke up from surgery, my right arm was in a bright pink cast from the top of my shoulder to the tips of my fingers. When I came home, the cast had to be tied to my power chair to prevent the weight of it from pulling me over. For six weeks, I needed help with everything. Instead of transferring into bed with minimal assistance, my parents lifted me. I bathed and washed my hair in bed. Once the cast was removed, I began the process of regaining range of motion and strengthening the muscle. In occupational therapy, I learned how to contract the muscle and use it as a tricep. I raised my right hand above my head for the first time in ten years.

I underwent three more surgeries, each followed by four weeks in a cast and several weeks of occupational therapy. Those surgeries gave me a pinch in both thumbs, using the brachioradialis muscles, and the ability to grip with my left hand, using my middle wrist muscle. I could pick up a book, grab a water bottle with my left hand, and securely hold silverware and makeup brushes without using adaptive devices. I was even able to confidently hold a bouquet of flowers as I rolled down the aisle as a maid of honor at Matthew and Misty's wedding that year.

The Christmas following the surgeries I decided to test my new dexterity. I grabbed wrapping paper, tape, a knife, and the presents I had purchased for my family. Sitting at the kitchen table, I figured out how to fold the wrapping paper and slice it with a knife along the creased edge. Folding the paper and using an abundance of tape, I managed to slowly wrap each item until I had a small pile of Christmas gifts for my family.

I've made this an annual tradition, not because wrapping Christmas presents is a major life skill, but because it's a symbol of the gift I was given by Dr. Shaw. Transferring independently in and out of bed, fastening my bra, typing and writing with my pinch or grip, grabbing a pan and spatula to cook dinner . . . these are the gifts of independence that wrapping presents remind me to be thankful for.

As for the scars I was so worried about? They are barely visible, thanks to Dr. Shaw's skill and attention to my concerns.

CHAPTER FOURTEEN

During one of my internships for counseling in 1998, I met two interns from Poland. David and Magda attended our weekly staff meetings, and I enjoyed chatting with them. As we lingered in the conference room after a meeting, I began asking questions about their country.

"What is life like for individuals with disabilities in Poland? How do people get to school and work?" I naïvely asked.

"A lot of people don't even have wheelchairs," David said.

"So what do they do?" In my tiny corner of the planet Earth, I had simply received a wheelchair upon my injury, and insurance covered the expense. Actually, I had received two wheelchairs: a power chair and a manual chair. I just assumed that was how it worked for everyone with a disability.

"Well, most people just stay home. But there's an organization that gives chairs to people in Poland who need them," Magda answered in her thick accent.

Being involved with an organization like that sounded like something I would love to do. I didn't have time since I was still in grad school, but the conversation planted a seed.

One year later, in 1999, I was reading the weekly bulletin at church when my eyes focused on a prayer request about a man from our congregation who was going to Afghanistan to distribute wheelchairs. I got his contact information and gave Tim a call.

Tim shared with me his passion for Afghanistan, a country most people hadn't even heard of before September 2001.

"After so many years of war, many people need wheelchairs, but there are few available. We'll be working with a nonprofit organization to give wheelchairs to people who don't have one. I can put you in touch with them if you'd like more information."

I was definitely interested. Several weeks later, I got a call from the vice president of the Mobility Project.

"Tim said you were interested in getting involved."

He explained how the organization collected wheelchairs people no longer used and refurbished them. They partnered with organizations in countries where there was a need. About 180 wheelchairs, along with walkers, canes, and crutches were shipped in a container, while a team of physical therapists and other volunteers traveled overseas to fit each wheelchair for the person who received it.

"We take our trash and turn it into gold for someone."

"How can I help?" I asked.

"We're going to Mexico. Why don't you come with us?"

I nearly choked. I had traveled by plane a few times in the United States, but it was with the support and physical assistance from my family.

Me? Go out of the country? That's impossible!

But my God is the God of the impossible.

~

Six months later, in February 2000, I was boarding a plane for Mexico City with Brenda, a nurse who offered to travel and assist me with my personal care. To get on the airplane, I had help transferring out of my manual wheelchair into an aisle chair provided by the airport; an aisle chair is a very narrow rolling seat that barely squeezes through the aisle of a plane. Straps crisscrossed my chest and secured my legs together as airport personnel maneuvered me backward onto the airplane. With assistance, I transferred into my assigned seat where I had placed my cushion to protect my bottom. My wheelchair was stowed in the belly of the plane and returned to the jetway after the flight.

In the Mexico City airport, I was overwhelmed as I heard Spanish spoken everywhere, confused by the immigration and customs process, and overrun by people wanting to push me or help with my luggage. Brenda and I found the others in our group and made our way to the bus. We were the only ones from Louisville, so we briefly greeted the ten team members from Colorado, Arizona, and Washington.

Steve, the president of the organization, and Chip, a volunteer from Colorado, asked how I preferred to be picked up. I explained one person should stand behind me and lift me under my shoulders, while the other should lift me under my knees. I could tell this wasn't their first time assisting someone with a disability as they went to their assigned places. I counted to three, and they lifted and carried me onboard, placing me on my cushion in the front seat. The bus took us to Toluca, a city about two hours west of Mexico City.

Since the house where we were staying was not occupied, I had received an email instructing volunteers to bring sleeping bags. But I wasn't prepared to find an empty house with no furniture or beds. I was actually going to sleep on the floor with six other women in a dining room with a curtain for a "door." We found a large piece of foam to put under my sleeping bag to prevent me from developing pressure sores from the hard tile floor. Volunteers stepped in to lift me every night from my chair to the sleeping bag and reversed the process each morning.

The bathroom was too small for me to enter, so I used a Sprite bottle to empty my catheter bag for the duration of the trip. I brushed my teeth and spit into a cup that Brenda rinsed for me, and I bathed with a wet washcloth and washed my hair with a water hose in the yard. As for the bowel program, I was too embarrassed to mention it to the group, so two of the nights I stayed at the house during the evening meal while the others ate out so I could have some privacy while "taking care of business" with Brenda's help; they brought us food on the two nights we didn't join them.

On the first day of distribution, Lisa, who was in charge of administration, assigned me to help with registration. We were in a town called San Bartolo Morelos, at an altitude of 8,500 feet in the gorgeous mountains of the Sierra Madre. Because of my ignorance of the need to hydrate properly at high altitude, I had a terrible headache.

I sat at the registration table with Linda, who had polio and also used a wheelchair. Each person in need of mobility, one after another, told us their name, or the name of their family member, as they arrived. I flipped through the large pile of applications until I found the corresponding request for a wheelchair. I let Lisa know when a recipient was in the waiting area. Family members often carried their disabled relative into the building. One woman, who was dressed in the colorful traditional clothing of the area, carried her eighteen-year-old son who had cerebral palsy. As I read through his application with my limited Spanish, I learned he had never had a wheelchair, and I realized, *This mother has been carrying her son for eighteen years.*

When registration slowed, I watched the three teams of volunteers work with wheelchair recipients in the "seating station." Volunteers used a measuring tape to check the width from hip to hip and the length from the back of the hips to just under the knee of each recipient to make sure the wheelchair was the right size. The volunteers examined each recipient to see if they needed additional trunk support, head support, or cushions. Did they have a pressure sore? A wheelchair must fit properly, otherwise it can cause more harm than good. Pressure sores, poor posture, or scoliosis can be caused by a wheelchair that isn't right for a person.

The mother who had carried her eighteen-year-old son that morning pushed him home in a wheelchair that afternoon. Both had received the precious gift of mobility I'd rarely thought twice about before that day.

The next day at a distribution in Toluca, I met Fabrina, who was dressed in her Sunday best. As I chatted with her, sometimes using an interpreter, I learned she had osteogenesis imperfecta, often called brittle bone disease. I watched as the volunteers adjusted a chair for her. Getting to know each person's story made the experience personal. We weren't just giving "someone" a wheelchair; we gave sixteen-year-old Fabrina a wheelchair.

In each city, the First Lady, the wife of the mayor, held a news conference with great fanfare. It was her job to represent the social welfare agency for Mexican families in their area known as DIF (Desarrollo Integral de la Familia). DIF was the partnering organization that had prepared the applications and was available for follow up.

On the third day, in Villa Guerrero, we distributed wheelchairs under a clear blue sky in the town square bursting in color with trees and blooming flowers. As a farming community, Villa Guerrero was lush with vegetation, unlike the other cities we had visited. About twenty mothers held their children with profound disabilities as they waited to receive wheelchairs. When I asked the First Lady if there was an explanation for so many children with disabilities, she told me the community believed it was from the pesticides used for farming.

By midafternoon, while the distribution was still taking place, school let out, and I suddenly had an audience of children dressed in uniforms who wanted to talk with the wheelchair-using *gringa*. Using my high school and college Spanish, I carried on brief conversations with the students, asking their ages and what they were studying. They giggled when I shrugged my shoulders and shook my head when I didn't understand their questions. It was a huge realization that I could barely speak or understand the Spanish that I had learned to read and write in school.

That evening we ate at an outdoor restaurant with flowering vines decorating the dining area. An older waitress came to our table and asked Steve if I'd be willing to talk with her husband.

"Why does she want me to talk with her husband?"

"She sees a joy in you that her husband doesn't have," Steve explained since I hadn't understood her question in Spanish. "He suffered a stroke several months ago and doesn't have any hope. She wants you to share your hope with him."

A thousand thoughts rushed through my mind. *What do I have that can give him hope?* Yes, I understood the hopelessness and frustration that occurs after a disability, but I had access to resources that he couldn't even imagine. I pushed myself over to this man, praying for wisdom as I went.

I sat face-to-face and chair-to-chair with the gentleman, in his late sixties, who acknowledged my approach with a crooked grin and nod of his head, while cradling his useless left arm in his lap. I told him the story of my injury. I spoke in Spanish and used an interpreter when my Spanish failed me. I then shared my hope.

"Hebrews 6:19 says, 'We have this hope as an anchor for the soul, firm and secure.' When everything around me was changing after my injury, God was the one I knew I could count on. He was always there. *He* is my hope and my strength."

With tears in his eyes, the man nodded in understanding. I asked if I could pray with him. Reaching out his right, non-paralyzed hand to me, he said, "*Sí, por favor.*"

After four days of distributions, we had a free day. The group traveled by bus to the ancient Aztec city of Teotihuacan. As an archaeology and history nerd, I sat in my chair, taking in my surroundings, mouth agape. Needless to say, ancient ruins were not created for wheelchairs, with their bumpy, uneven slabs of stone and pebble walkways. But I was with a group of people who were willing to help me enjoy the day. Five of them decided to go up the Pyramid of the Sun.

"Do you want to go?" Steve asked. "We'll get you up the steps."

I looked at Brenda. "Want to try this?"

She nodded and laughed at my willingness to attempt the unthinkable.

With Steve holding the push handles on the back of my manual chair and Chip grabbing the front of the frame, they bumped me and my chair up each hand-hewn step, uneven in depth and height. As we scaled the steps of the pyramid, I could hear the men inhaling deeply while I tried to keep my balance and looked out over the Avenue of the Dead, the walkway between the two largest pyramids. We reached the second level after ascending more than one hundred steps. During the brief breather, Steve took a picture of Brenda and me as proof that we'd actually been more than halfway up a pyramid.

"Okay, Jenny, we're ready. Let's keep going," Steve said.

I turned around and looked up the incline of the steps that was even steeper and longer than what we had just ascended. I also listened to the guys still breathing heavily from their exertion.

"I think we've come high enough. It's not that I don't trust you. But we still have to get back down!"

That's impossible.

I had said these words before going to Mexico. I thought they were true until I applied mascara for the first time after my injury. I believed them before I started driving, when Terri encouraged me to participate in the pageant, and until I had the tendon transfer surgeries. In each situation, I learned that what I assumed to be impossible was possible.

But first, I had to try. I needed to say yes. I had to take a risk and get out of my comfort zone, because the impossible rarely happens where it's safe and comfortable.

It's a lesson I need to learn again and again.

CHAPTER FIFTEEN

A few months after I returned from Mexico, I was at the salon as my stylist used a spray bottle to dampen my hair since transferring to a seat by the sink to wash my hair was too much hassle. She said, "I was talking with a client, and you came up in our conversation."

An article about Ms. Wheelchair Kentucky in the local newspaper caught the eye of Judi Petty. "Judi plays tennis and is interested in coaching wheelchair tennis. She'd be willing to meet with you sometime if you're interested."

Tennis? It had been more than ten years since my injury, and I hadn't tried playing sports. As a not-yet-recovering perfectionist, my theory was if I couldn't play sports well, then I shouldn't play at all.

"Go ahead and give her my number," I heard myself say.

The first time Judi and I met for tennis was in the driveway at my parents' house. I sat in my manual wheelchair with a Velcro strap fastened around my abdomen to keep me from falling forward. Even when I wasn't playing sports, it was possible to lose my balance without the use of my stomach and back muscles. Judi wrapped athletic tape around my fingers and the tennis racket allowing me to "grasp" the racket with my right hand. I pushed my chair lopsidedly to the middle of the driveway since my left hand was free, but my right hand held the racket, and I lined up across from Judi.

"Ready?" Judi asked.

I nodded.

She tossed a foam Nerf ball in my direction. I swung the racket and missed the ball by a foot.

I thumped my racketed right hand against the push rim of my chair in frustration.

"Keep your eye on the ball and swing a bit sooner this time."

Focused intensely on the yellow foam ball, I pulled my arm behind me, swung as the ball neared, made contact, and the ball rebounded into the air. It didn't soar but ten feet, but it was a start.

In two weeks, we met at the public tennis courts near my house. Although it took a few weeks of practice to get the timing of pushing my chair and swinging the racket coordinated, once I consistently connected with the ball, I experienced a rush at the sound of the ball popping off the sweet spot of the racket and felt the power generated through my arm as the ball soared over the net.

I had a physical outlet again.

After completing my master's and healing from the surgeries on my arms, it was time to get a job.

A year earlier when I was having the tendon transfers, I looked for volunteer opportunities while I recuperated. I heard about the need for volunteers in the school system's adult English as a Second Language program. Between surgeries, I tutored English three hours a week to immigrants and refugees. As I taught lessons, I carried on brief conversations in English with students, sometimes their first opportunity to speak in English without fear or judgment, and I saw their eyes light up in understanding. With the more advanced students, I listened as they told me about their cultures, so vastly different from mine.

When I returned from Mexico, I started to look for teaching or tutoring positions in ESL. Despite passing the state's certification exam as a masters-level psychologist, I still had no desire to be a therapist. The public school system hired me as a part-time ESL teacher for kindergarten through fifth grade. Because of the shortage of ESL teachers, the school system waived the requirement of being certified as a teacher and "emergency certified" me for one year. It was an ideal situation since I was teaching only four hours a day, which made the transition to work less overwhelming, and gave me the chance to lie down each afternoon for an hour to keep my bottom in good shape.

In the classroom I shared with another ESL teacher, I sat at a round table and worked with groups of three to four students at a time. I left the school each day with my heart full after seeing students laugh when they understood a joke or upon hearing the appreciation in the parents' voices for their children's education.

In the middle of that school year, in December 2000, I requested a week off to go on my second trip with the Mobility Project for a tennis and sports camp for people with disabilities in Mazatlán, Mexico. Since I had just been introduced to wheelchair tennis, the timing seemed more than coincidental.

The sports camp started after Richard, the sports director for the Mobility Project, vacationed at Torres Mazatlán, on the west coast of Mexico. As an accomplished adapted skier and wheelchair tennis player, Richard signed up for some court time with the tennis pro, Roberto. Surprised by Richard's injury, Roberto told him he wasn't able to play tennis because he used a wheelchair. Did I mention Richard had been a lawyer? No one tells Rich what he can't do. He asked Roberto again for the opportunity to play, and Roberto gave in. With one well-played tennis match, Rich convinced the tennis pro that a wheelchair user was quite capable of playing tennis.

Rich's experience that day led to a discussion with the hotel management about hosting a tennis clinic for residents of Mazatlán with disabilities. Would the hotel welcome wheelchair users to play tennis on their courts? It would, and the Mazatlán tennis camp was born. The hotel graciously has hosted the event every year.

In full disclosure, during the Mazatlán camp, we stayed at Torres Mazatlán, a four-star property of Vacation Internationale —a far cry from sleeping on the hard floor of an empty house in Toluca. Palm trees lined the tennis courts while a grassy area with thatch-roofed *palapas*, or open-sided shaded dwellings, provided easy access to view the beach for those of us who used wheelchairs. Every evening after a long day on the courts, we munched on chips and salsa as we watched the sun set over the Pacific. It was really roughing it for Jesus.

Throughout the four days of camp, six instructors—all wheelchair tennis players from the US—led the group of twenty participants through stretches, movement drills, forehand and backhand strokes, and serving. Every day ended with a ruthless game of Sharks and Minnows, where one shark attacked the minnows until a single minnow was left "standing." Throughout the camp, I was a participant alongside the local wheelchair users as we learned to play tennis and even some basketball. As needed, I handed out and collected nametags at the registration table with Lisa or counted the number of volunteers and participants who would be eating lunch.

After going out for dinner one evening, I arrived back at the hotel, and Steve told me my mom had left a message at the front desk requesting I call home.

"My mom wouldn't call unless something's wrong."

"Oh, she probably just wants to check on you," Steve said.

I made a collect call to my parents' landline since cellphones and Wi-Fi were still a thing of the future.

"What's going on?" I said as soon as my mom answered.

After a few seconds, she said, "Kevin died in a motorcycle accident in California."

Her words knocked the wind out of me. Kevin, one of the guys from the band, had pushed me beyond my comfort zone from the beginning of my injury; he was one of the reasons I was daring enough to go to Mexico. It'd been several years since we had spoken, but the role he'd played in my life never faded.

"When's the service?" I asked.

"They don't know yet."

I pondered for a moment, "If it's before Sunday, let me know."

We said our goodbyes, and I went to sit alone near the beach. I needed to be by myself and think. Or maybe feel. Kevin was the first person close to me who had died. I didn't know how to process the grief. I allowed the sound of the waves to wash over me as I wiped away tears.

Back in my room, I laid in bed reading my Bible, searching for comfort. For answers. I remembered the words that were embedded in my heart from a song we played in the band. First Corinthians 15:54-55 (NLT) says:

> Then, when our dying bodies have been transformed into bodies that will never die, this Scripture will be fulfilled:
> "Death is swallowed up in victory.
> O death, where is your victory?
> O death, where is your sting?"

In my human heart, death stung. But I knew Kevin was where "there will be no more death or mourning or crying or pain" (Rev. 21:4 NIV).

My mom called again to let me know Kevin's funeral was scheduled after I would return to Louisville. Gathering with friends, including Scott and David, gave me the opportunity to remember my friend who had helped me see that my injury didn't have to stop me from living adventurously and with laughter.

After the sports camp, I returned to teaching ESL, but near the end of the school year, I had to take a leave of absence. Despite my best efforts at pressure relief and getting in bed religiously every afternoon, I had another small pressure sore develop on my bottom since scar tissue isn't as durable as the original skin. From my past experience, I knew I needed to stay in bed for at least several weeks.

I had surgery again in 2001.

Thankfully, since then my butt has been surgery-free. I have to be vigilant, though. I learned the hard way that my bottom is my most valuable *asset* (pun totally intended).

Today, the very first thing I do when I get in bed each night, after I undress, is grab a mirror and look at my bottom. If there's any sign of redness, I have to stay in bed the next day and get up only a few times for two hours. Fear motivates me to stay in bed—even when it's inconvenient—because I now understand that a few days in bed is better than months and months of bed rest and surgery.

While recovering from the third skin flap surgery, I received a call from Steve, the president of the Mobility Project.

"Would you consider working for us as a regional coordinator?" he asked. "It's some of what you've already been doing: collecting wheelchairs in your area, doing administration, getting the word out to the public, and helping with overseas distributions."

My heart skipped a beat thinking about doing this as *my job*. But I knew there was a catch.

"I'd have to raise support?" I asked, already knowing the answer since Steve and Lisa raised their salaries from donors.

"Yep."

A support-based position requires asking individuals and churches to donate money for salary and business expenses. I had friends already working in support-based positions, so it wasn't a totally foreign concept. When Steve called, I was trying to make the decision whether to pursue a second master's degree so I could continue teaching.

Really God? My choices are either to raise support or to get another degree?

Raising financial support would require trusting God to provide for my financial needs through others. It was intimidating to rely on others and not on my own effort. But the opportunity to tangibly change the lives of people with disabilities in other countries seemed to be an opportunity too good to pass up simply because I was scared. I'd seen with my own eyes —and experienced myself—the difference a wheelchair makes in a person's life.

After a lot of prayer, I said yes and decided to work with the Mobility Project.

CHAPTER SIXTEEN

Six months after the sports camp, I returned to Mexico for a month to assist with two volunteer groups coming from California and Washington. I stayed and worked out of Misión Mazahua, an eighteenth-century hacienda in the heart of where the indigenous Mazahua people live. The cobblestone walkways, stone walls, gardens, and the old chapel sit at an altitude of 10,000 feet. The weather in San Felipe del Progreso warmed up nicely in the summer sun, but the evenings were downright cold.

My mom and cousin Elizabeth joined me for the first part of the trip. On one particularly damp and chilly evening, we added layers of clothing, but we still were shivering. To take the chill out of the air in our room, we turned on the gas oven for a bit.

The first morning of the wheelchair distribution, with chairs and other mobility aids lined up along the main outdoor walkway through Misión Mazahua, the first group of volunteers was ready to start the outreach. The organization's staff, which now included me, explained how to adjust each wheelchair, while only people with experience worked on more complicated seatings, such as pediatric wheelchairs. The staff at Misión Mazahua had found the people who needed wheelchairs and collected the applications. We distributed about sixty wheelchairs that week. One of the recipients was Mara, a twenty-three-year-old college student studying New and Old Testament at a local school. Her small frame and limp arms hid the fact that she was a powerhouse to be reckoned with. Her parents obviously valued learning and hadn't allowed her disability to prevent her from getting an education since it was common for children with disabilities to be banned from school, either out of shame from having a disability or lack of access. Mara's determination to live life was another example to me that we shouldn't set limits on ourselves or others.

After my mom and cousin left, Lisa, Steve, another couple, and I stayed in a house in San Bartolo Morelos that Lisa and I dubbed "the cave." The house was dark and cold with mud-brick walls. It was equipped with furniture that seemed to be built for exceptionally small people. Lisa and I often sat outside since it was the only way to get warm, but the strong sun left me sunburned almost daily.

The house needed a serious makeover, especially since Steve was getting married in a few months and planned to live with Miriam in the house after their wedding. Lisa and I wanted his wife to spend her first few months of marriage in a more comfortable home, so we made the hour-and-a-half drive to Toluca to shop at Carrefour, a large discount department store, for new sheets and curtains. We did our best to fix up the house before Miriam's arrival.

In the back of the house was a spacious room with orange

walls and plastic lawn chairs. It served as a classroom. Twice a day I taught English; one class for about twenty kids at ten o'clock in the morning. and one for ten adults at five o'clock in the evening. It was a very basic class, and I struggled to come up with lesson plans, but I built relationships with the community. On the last day of class, the students showered me with confetti, and I received several gifts. The blue ceramic mugs with yellow sunflowers I received from two sisters still sit in my kitchen.

While I was in San Bartolo Morelos, I hired a local woman to help me with personal care for the first time in Mexico. Rosaba assisted me with the bowel program a few nights a week and helped me get dressed each morning. I apologized as I grappled for words in Spanish, but she was patient and a good teacher as we conversed in Spanish. Rosaba was generous with her time, energy, and knowledge throughout her visits. She told me about her community and life in Mexico. On future trips, I frequently hired locals to assist with my personal care after this positive experience.

That summer was hard. It felt long. Each cobblestone jarred me to my core as I pushed over the bumpy surfaces at Misión Mazahua. Staying in the cold, dark house in San Bartolo Morelos, I was chilled to the bone. I had to remind myself I couldn't get through the summer on my own strength. I clung to one verse during those four weeks. Zechariah 4:6 (NIV) says: "'Not by might nor by power, but by my Spirit,' says the Lord Almighty."

It's still a lesson I have to practice every day, no matter where in the world I might be.

∾

In December 2001, I returned to Mazatlán for a wheelchair distribution and sports camp. We distributed twenty-five wheelchairs, then had the sports camp and gave fifteen ultralight chairs like I used every day, as well as specially designed tennis chairs, to the camp participants. A tennis chair has cambered, or angled, wheels to increase the stability and the ease of turning the chair while playing tennis. Each sport has a wheelchair designed specifically for it, just like there are tennis shoes, soccer cleats, cross-trainers, running shoes, and other sports shoes.

Waiting in the airport for my return flight to the US, I wrote the following as I pondered the past year:

As I sit in the airport in Mexico City during a two-hour layover, I am amazed as to what God can do. Here I am, sitting in Mexico City all by myself, ordering french fries and a Sprite in Spanish. I really just want to laugh out loud. Who would have imagined—even before my injury—that I would be in this scene? "With man this is impossible, but not with God; all things are possible with God." (Mark 10:27 NIV)

I returned from Mexico and focused on collecting used mobility equipment from individuals, nursing homes, and durable medical supply companies in my area, which would be refurbished in Iowa before being donated overseas. I also made a one-week trip to Mexico to join a group of cadets from the Air Force Academy for a wheelchair distribution. A high schooler from my area, Alan Sea, who has cerebral palsy, joined us on that trip; he had collected mobility equipment in Lexington, Kentucky, as a project for his bar mitzvah.

As summer neared, I assisted Lisa with organizing the schedule and plans for the summer groups. In the summer of

2002, I spent six weeks in Santa Clara, another small town in the mountains of Mexico. Since Lisa lived in the Seattle area, we seized the opportunity when we could work in person to refine the administrative aspects of the organization. Lisa had learned to help me with my bowel program and was willing to assist when necessary, but I hired Magaly that summer. As I spent time with her and her sister, Vieneth, they told me their hopes and dreams; dreams that weren't much different from my own. Magaly told me of her love for animals and how she studied hard in school since she wanted to become a veterinarian. In the years since then, she has done just that. I still hated needing help, but I was beginning to see the benefit of learning the culture and speaking the language as much as possible. It was a ministry opportunity the able-bodied staff didn't have. I also was able to provide a paying job to someone in the community.

The city of Santa Clara was small and tranquil. The house where we stayed was spacious and . . . active. At night I could hear critters running above me in the ceiling. I'd tuck myself deep into the heavy blankets and cover my head, more for protection of the unknown than the cold. Neighbors often burned trash outside the house. Whenever I smell a fire burning outdoors, my mind immediately returns to that house and its trash pile. I'd wake up to the sound of birds, roosters, and burros (and a few sick-sounding dogs) every morning. Not being a country girl, I learned in Mexico that roosters do not cock-a-doodle-doo just one time each morning like in the movies, but again and again and again. Dumb things.

The women who prepared dinner every night for the teams were wonderful cooks. I ate and ate. Tortas, beans, rice, *papas fritas* fried outdoors over a fire in a large cast-iron kettle, roasted chicken, and *guayaba* tea were some of the delicious foods I enjoyed.

Getting to know the people, trying to understand the culture, experiencing the slower pace of life, and savoring the fresh food, this was the Mexico I fell in love with.

CHAPTER SEVENTEEN

In early 2003, Mobility Project staff and volunteers were at the municipal palace in San José, Costa Rica. The sterile government building had little natural light and felt dark despite being covered with creamy white marble tile. The chattering from wheelchair recipients and volunteers echoed off the stone walls. Although this country was more developed than others in Central America, about thirty children, men, and women with disabilities who needed wheelchairs, sat in folding metal chairs designated as a waiting area.

Someone called my name over the clatter, and I turned my chair in their direction. A volunteer motioned for me to come over.

"Could you help us with our next recipient? We need an interpreter. And I think you can help us with this fitting too."

"Sure," I said, pushing my way to the seating station, which was fully supplied with all the screwdrivers, wrenches, hammers, pipe cutters, and other tools necessary to adjust a wheelchair to properly fit an individual.

When I got to the seating station, I saw a young woman

who appeared to be about my age sitting on the floor. She smiled at me. Her thin legs, arms, and hands were atrophied just like mine. Two family members sat on either side of her.

"Hi, I'm Jenny," I said in Spanish. "What's your name?"

"I'm Maribel."

"It's nice to meet you, Maribel. What level spinal cord injury do you have?" I asked, assuming she had sustained an injury.

"I had polio," Maribel responded.

My mouth dropped open. She seemed young, yet had had polio. "Really? And how old are you?"

"I'm forty-three."

I wouldn't have guessed she was more than ten years older than me; I was thirty. But her age explained why she had polio; the disease wasn't eradicated in Costa Rica until 1973.

"Do you have a wheelchair?"

"No."

I interpreted the conversation for the volunteer, who wrote down the information for the organization's records.

"How do you get around your house?" I asked.

Glancing at the men in our group and the woman taking notes, Maribel lowered her tear-filled eyes to the ground. "*En mi trasero.*"

On my bottom.

The shame with which she said these three words cut me to the core. Although I had heard hundreds of people say those same words in the past three years, hearing it from Maribel moved me to tears.

Why, Lord? Why?

Why polio? Why did she not have a chair since childhood? But I also struggled with another question: *Why me? Why did I have a wheelchair and she did not?*

As the volunteers took measurements—the width of Maribel's hips and the length from the back of her hips to just under her knees—we chatted about her family and support system. Once the volunteers had her measurements, I went with them to look through the dozens of wheelchairs lined up against the far wall for one that would fit her.

Going from chair to chair, I looked at the tags tied to the push handle of each wheelchair indicating its width and length. With limited upper body function, Maribel would need removable armrests to make transfers easier. I hoped to find a chair with plastic-coated handrims to make pushing easier with no hand function, but we didn't have any. My heart ached that I couldn't get a custom-fit lightweight wheelchair for Maribel. In the United States, I had selected every aspect of my chair—even the color—to my exact specification: an aluminum or titanium frame, a custom backrest for improved posture, a cushion to prevent skin breakdown, as well as dozens of other options. But for Maribel, we had a limited selection. We found the narrowest chair available with the appropriate length. A volunteer pushed it over to the seating station.

Maribel transferred to the chair with assistance from her family members. After we adjusted the height of the footplates where her feet rested, it looked like a good fit.

"Does it feel okay?" I asked.

She nodded.

"Let me show you how to push the chair."

We lined up side by side. "I use the heel of my hand to push," I said, demonstrating. "Now you try."

After a few attempts, Maribel moved the chair. She was pushing a wheelchair for the first time. A satisfied smile appeared on her face.

The volunteer handed me a piece of paper with instructions

in Spanish about how to do pressure relief, take care of one's skin, and maintain the wheelchair.

"Every thirty minutes you need to relieve the pressure from your bottom so you don't get a pressure sore. This is how I do it."

Placing my hands on the top of my push rims, I lifted my body with my arms so my bottom was off my cushion. "Twenty seconds, okay? If you can't lift, you can lean from side to side like this." I hooked my left arm around the push handle of my chair and leaned over to my right side until my right hand could almost touch the floor.

I interpreted as the volunteers showed her and the family how to fold the chair, place it in a car, and how to go up and down steps safely when ramps were not available.

Maribel pushed her new chair over to me and leaned in. "Could I have a table like that one to place my Bible on?" She motioned to a removable tray that another wheelchair recipient had on their chair.

"Definitely!"

Maribel and I took a moment to have our picture taken together. I've met hundreds, maybe thousands, of people during wheelchair distributions, but few people stand out in my mind as much as Maribel. Maybe it was her age or our similar disabilities. I think we would've been dear friends had we lived in the same city or state.

I cherish that picture of Maribel; it personifies a changed life. It's the reason I was willing to continuously raise funding, put up with inaccessible accommodations, and be carried on and off buses. Those temporary hardships were worth it because Maribel had the opportunity to experience hope, dignity, and independence that she wouldn't have had without a wheelchair.

~

When I wasn't traveling, Judi and I continued to get together regularly to play tennis for the next two years. I was hooked. Not only were my strength and pushing abilities improving, but I had a physical outlet again to reduce stress and eliminate the day's frustrations. When I played tennis, the world's problems disappeared. All that was on my mind was pushing the chair, swinging the racket, and hitting the ball.

When I went to the second sports camp in Mazatlán two years earlier, I met some incredible volunteers. I had a blast going out to dinner with the group of chair users. Our dinner conversations often revolved around bladder and bowel function and other daily goings-on of life with a chair. As the only female with a disability in the group, it was quite an eye-opening experience to talk so openly about the physical aspects of a spinal cord injury that I'd only had the chance to discuss with the women at the Ms. Wheelchair America pageant. I was grateful to have another female volunteer, Bree, join us on the male-dominated outings.

Michael Cottingham, a wheelchair tennis coach at the University of Arizona, was there to volunteer. He had been the first wheelchair athlete to be offered a scholarship to play tennis at the university level. He encouraged me to come to Tucson to play in a tennis tournament he was hosting. I decided to go.

I still was playing in my everyday manual chair at that first tournament in March 2003, since even a low-end tennis chair costs thousands of dollars. Bree met me in Arizona to assist with personal care.

After the first day of matches, Bree and I agreed to meet in the room at ten thirty for my nighttime routine. Tired and sore, I waited in the hotel room. I got anxious as the minutes ticked by. After sitting up all day, I really needed to get off my bottom. Plus, the matches started again early the next day. I called her cell phone. She didn't answer. I texted. No reply. Half an hour passed and, feeling frustrated, I threw what I needed on the bed, got the sliding board, and decided to transfer into bed on my own. I knew I was capable of transferring by myself, but I always wanted someone nearby . . . just in case. I didn't want to risk falling. But on this night, I needed to take that risk.

I lined my chair up next to the bed, slipped the sliding board under my legs, and using my upper body, lifted and moved myself into the hotel bed.

Whew. I made it.

I hooked my right wrist under my knee and lifted my leg into bed using my bicep and repeated with my left leg. Once I was completely in bed, I bent my left knee by pulling my leg up with my arm and crossed my ankle over my right leg so I could reach my foot. Slowly, I wedged my shoe off using the palm of my hand, then pulled off my sock. I repeated the same strategy with my right side. Looking at the clock, I couldn't believe Bree wasn't in the room yet to help me. Where was she? Why wouldn't she answer her phone?

I slid my thumb into the waistband of my pants. Rolling from side to side, I slowly wiggled and tugged my pants down until each foot was free. I needed to switch my catheter bag, which I'd never been able to do, or had never taken enough time to try to do. Millimeter by millimeter, I scooted the Foley catheter off the end of my leg bag, then pushed the tip of the night bag into the catheter so the urine could drain into it.

I did it.

I started bawling. Fourteen years into my spinal cord injury and this was the first time I had ever independently completed my nighttime routine.

I heard the doorknob turn, and Bree walked through the door. She saw the tears streaming down my face and anxiously asked, "Jenny, what's wrong?"

"I . . . did . . . it," I sobbed. "I didn't know I could do it. Why didn't I know I could do it after all these years?"

Either out of guilt or relief, Bree started crying too. "Mike took my phone away from me and wouldn't let me leave," she told me. "He said you'd do it on your own if I didn't come up."

At the time, I was more angry at Mike than grateful. His technique had infuriated me, but I can laugh about it now. It was exactly what I needed. It was something no one—not my parents, personal care attendants, or therapists—had ever done. Mike put me in a situation where I *had* to do it by myself.

By the next day, word had spread around at the tournament, and players fist-bumped and congratulated me. The attention was embarrassing, but encouraging as well. Their lessons and "tricks of the trade" were pushing me to a new level of independence. More possibilities.

After returning home to Louisville, I quietly closed my bedroom door at my parents' house, put my stuff on the bed, and gave it another try. I did it again. No falling when I transferred. No end-of-the-world disasters. Just another glimpse of independence that I had never imagined for myself.

At age thirty, I could finally go to bed at whatever time I wanted.

CHAPTER EIGHTEEN

Tim, the man from my church who introduced me to the Mobility Project, had a passion for the Afghan people that was contagious. And I caught the bug.

For years Afghanistan had been riddled by war and controlled by the Taliban. The political situation in Afghanistan became a bit more realistic to me in August 2001, when Dayna Curry, Heather Mercer, and six of their co-workers were arrested by the Taliban. They were working for a non-governmental organization (NGO) in Afghanistan called Shelter Now International. I prayed for them daily.

As I began learning about the history of the country and praying for its people, I wondered where I fit into this situation. When a wheelchair distribution was planned for Pakistan to provide wheelchairs to Afghan refugees in late 2001, I committed to going.

Then the terrorist attacks of September 11, 2001, happened.

The trip to Pakistan was canceled.

It wasn't until November 15, after three months of imprisonment, that the Shelter Now aid workers were released from prison and rescued by the United States military.

In the year following 9/11, the number of international NGOs in Afghanistan tripled. The Mobility Project planned a wheel-chair distribution in Afghanistan in early 2003, and Lisa went on that trip.

"Let me know if it's doable. I want to go next time if you think it's possible," I told her before she left.

On her return, Lisa called. "You can do this, Jen. Physically, it's not much different than Mexico."

Getting around physically was where the similarities between Mexico and Afghanistan ended, though.

Despite what would become six trips to Afghanistan, I have had only a very small taste of what Afghanistan is like. I was never in-country for more than three and a half weeks. And honestly, by the end of those three weeks, I was usually ready to return to my accessible and independent life in the US.

My heroes in Afghanistan are the many NGO workers and families who lived and served there for years—sometimes decades—throughout the fighting between the Soviets and *mujahideen*, and under the rule of the Taliban. More recently, the terrorist attacks have been aimed at Afghans and Westerners alike. I can't understand what it's like to live there as a *kharagi*, a foreigner. I haven't experienced the daily stressors, the loss of dear friends and family members, or the constant need for vigilance.

Afghanistan and I have a complicated love/hate relationship. I love the people and parts of the culture. But the difficulty getting around, the arid climate, the never-ending dust, the extreme temperatures, the culture that devalues women—these aspects of Afghanistan were difficult for me. However, the needs, especially of the disabled, drew me back again and again. The needs continue to pull at my heart.

Traveling to Afghanistan in and of itself is a feat.

In 2002, the United Nations lifted sanctions and allowed planes to fly into the country. What had been a long, arduous drive on gutted roads from Pakistan to Kabul over the Khyber Pass became a three-hour flight from Dubai to Kabul.

On August 28, 2003, I boarded a plane in Louisville and met Steve and his wife, Miriam, in Atlanta for a flight to London. Because of the long flights, I needed to break up the travel to ensure my bottom made it safely to our destination, so we overnighted in London and met Lisa at Gatwick Airport to fly to Dubai.

After deplaning in Dubai, I was separated from the others because the route to immigration and customs wasn't accessible. The airport was like a meeting of the world's nations: men dressed in long white robes with checkered *keffiyehs* adorning their heads; Indian women clothed in colorful saris; Europeans wore everything from business suits to jeans and T-shirts. The women covered in black from head to toe, including their faces, suffocated my freedom-craving nature. Although they were hidden, they were anything but invisible.

Lisa's luggage hadn't made it, and Miriam, who held a Mexican passport, needed a visa. It turned into a very, very long day. After several hours, we arrived at the hotel, and I got into bed while the others went shopping to replace missing clothing (Lisa's luggage didn't arrive for a week and a half). The next day, after a good night's rest in the hotel, we went to Terminal 2 of the Dubai airport. The women dressed in long, loose pants and knee-length tops with long sleeves, called a *shalwar chemise*. Around our necks hung head coverings, or *chadars*, ready to cover our heads once we were on the flight to Kabul.

Finally, we boarded an Ariana flight to Kabul. Ariana was better known as "Scary-ana." The airplanes were decommissioned Soviet and Indian aircraft that made noises that truly had me praying. In 2006 the European Union actually deemed the airline unworthy for safe travel.

As we neared Kabul, the remnants of war were evident even from the air; one side of the runway was littered with damaged planes and bombed-out tanks.

As expected, there was no aisle chair to help me get off the plane, nor was there a jetway to the airport.

"Ready to do this?" Steve asked.

"Let's do it."

Steve picked me up, carried me through the aisle of the plane, and set me in my chair on a platform leading to a flight of thirty steps that descended to the runway. With an audience of wide-eyed Afghan men watching our every move, step-by-step we descended the stairs until my wheels were finally on the ground in Afghanistan and I could push myself.

I'm fairly sure few, if any, of these men had ever seen a Western woman pushing a wheelchair.

As we made our way toward the immigration and customs building, airport personnel kept coming up behind me and pushing my chair. I know people mean well, but it can throw me off balance when someone pushes my chair without telling me first.

I need to learn how to say "Please don't push me" in Dari.

Inside the hot building, long-bearded men wearing shalwar chemises packed tightly in the receiving area. Some wore vests over their shalwar chemise; others added suit jackets to their ensemble, looking a bit more Western. In a small corner, women squatted beside their children with their burqas flipped backward, allowing their faces to show.

Once we were through customs and immigration, we found our luggage and met the representative of the nongovernmental organization with whom we were partnering. We piled in several vehicles and made our way to the guesthouse.

Behind a security wall and gated entrance, five steps led up into a comfortable two-story house that accommodated a number of NGO workers and volunteers from the US. The women in our group stayed on the ground level, sharing a single room with six twin beds equipped with decent mattresses.

I decided it was doable, just as Lisa had said.

One of our team members had a virus when she arrived. One by one, volunteers and nationals came down with a severe upper respiratory infection. By the second day, Lisa was running a 102-degree fever. By day three, Steve and Miriam were sick, as well as Mary. Eventually, the workers in the guesthouse caught it. I desperately prayed I wouldn't get sick, but I was the last one to succumb to the nasty bug on the fourth day in-country.

As I mentioned earlier, without the use of my abdominal and intercostal muscles, I don't have the ability to make a "productive cough." As my congestion worsened, I became concerned. Pneumonia can kill a quad, and I needed to take every precaution to prevent it. Thankfully, Stephany, a doctor of osteopathy, was also staying at the guesthouse.

"Let me listen to your lungs," she said. As she placed the stethoscope on my chest, I took a deep breath. "Your lungs still sound okay. Let's get you in bed, and we'll loosen things up."

I transferred into bed and turned onto my side. Two women placed the bed on some books so my head was lower than my feet.

"I'm going to do some chest percussions." Stephany rapidly thumped on my back and chest to loosen the congestion. I turned at her request, and she continued pounding. After several minutes, I sat up, grasping for anything within reach to help me lean into my diaphragm to force a cough and get up what needed to come out. It was exhausting.

Because of the illness, Lisa and I stayed at the guesthouse for the first several days while the others were out doing the scheduled activities. On top of the discomfort of my congestion, cough, and fever, the daytime temperature was ninety degrees. The city provided electricity only from about seven in the evening to four in the morning, and the guesthouse generators went out in the afternoon, so there weren't even fans to circulate the hot air.

With a spinal cord injury at the C6-7 level, my autonomic nervous system doesn't function, and my body is incapable of temperature regulation. I'm basically a cold-blooded animal. If it's hot outside, my body temperature will go up. If it's cold, my core body temperature will drop. It's hard to know if I was running a fever the entire trip or simply overheated. Either way, it was uncomfortable.

Lisa and I sat on the front porch of the guesthouse when I

noticed odd-colored clouds on the horizon. The wind picked up, and I realized the yellowish haze was a massive dust cloud heading our direction. I'd seen them before in Arizona. We quickly gathered our belongings, went inside, and pointed out the window to the staff. The guesthouse workers scurried to close all the windows and doors. For the next forty-five minutes, it rained. Kabul, in a drought-ridden country where even the Kabul River was running dry, needed rain. Recalling the song "Let it Rain" by Michael W. Smith, I went to my room and listened to it on my computer. While the song played, I prayed for the people and country of Afghanistan, while thanking God for the rain.

The next day, Lisa and I joined the others at the distribution site. Traffic in Afghanistan was quite an experience and would only worsen in the coming years. The smell of diesel fuel hung in the air. Men on bicycles, horse-drawn carts overflowing with merchandise, yellow taxis, ornately painted cargo trucks, and an occasional rickshaw carrying burqa-clad women drove on the same roads as white United Nations Toyota 4 Runners. Add the donkeys, boys herding sheep, and the massive army-green military vehicles and tanks, and you had the makings of chaos. And not organized chaos. After six trips to Afghanistan, the only semblance of a road rule I could decipher was to honk if the driver had no intention of stopping.

The van I had the "pleasure" of riding in had the steering wheel on the right side. It was one of many vehicles that had been imported from Pakistan, where people drive on the left side of the road. But in Afghanistan, people drive on the right. That made for what felt like a dangerous situation as our driver seemed to haphazardly decide to pass the vehicle in front of us, even though I could see vehicles speeding toward us before he could.

From the vehicle, we saw fruit and vegetable stands—selling imported bananas, apples, pomegranates, onions, and other produce—dotting the sides of the streets. Open-air butcher shops displayed their "fresh" merchandise. Warm *naan*, the flatbread that is a staple of every meal, was sold on almost every street corner. Young boys squatting on the side of the road sold chickens; I still don't know if those chickens were alive or dead. If alive, they were very well-behaved chickens. Boys and girls pumped water into plastics jugs and carried the heavy cargo back to their houses. Women in burqas and small children would come up to the window of the vehicle to beg. Not wanting to treat her as invisible, yet having been told to never give money, I simply reached out and touched one woman's hand in an effort to say, "I see you."

Tanks littered the sides of the road to Parwan, a province northwest of Kabul, where we held the wheelchair distributions. Some of the heaviest fighting with the Soviets occurred in this area, and the evidence was visible. Speed bumps were made out of old tank treads.

For the hour-and-a-half ride, I had nothing to grab onto to assist me in coughing. By the time we arrived at the distribution, I felt like I was drowning. It was a relief to be lifted out of the vehicle into my chair where I could clear my lungs.

I saw tarps hanging from trees that formed a divided waiting area for the distribution: one side for women, one side for the men. Men, women, and children arrived one by one, some hobbling on ill-fitting prosthetics, some carried by family members, some even pushed in wheelbarrows.

I pushed over to the women's waiting area, a large, open grassy area shaded from the bright sun by tall, skinny evergreen trees and shorter trees dense with leaves. Behind the privacy of the tarps, the women had flipped back their burqas, allowing us to see their faces.

The female volunteers in our group adjusted the wheelchairs for the Afghan women. My role was to tell the volunteers how to adjust each chair for it to fit properly.

"Pesta Gul?" my interpreter asked the group of women, reading the name on the first application.

A woman nodded and scooted on her bottom across the uncut grass to the seating station's "floor" of broken-down cardboard boxes. Through the interpreter, I learned that Pesta Gul's house had been bombed in 1997. She suffered injuries to her abdomen and right leg, as well as burns on her face that left significant scars. We took her measurements, chose a wheelchair, adjusted it to fit her, and explained how to maintain the chair, as well as how to prevent pressure sores.

Name after name was called, all with stories you don't hear on the nightly news. Farida, twenty-two, was paralyzed on one side since birth. Be Be Rahat was a widow at thirty-seven. A bomb fell on her house, and she lost her right leg at the hip, as well as her husband. Fifteen-year-old Ferishta was two when she became sick with an unknown illness. She was paralyzed after a doctor gave her an injection. Shukira was ten years old when she stepped on a land mine that blew off her leg while walking to Kabul.

During those ten days, the Mobility Project fitted and distributed about 130 wheelchairs for men, women, and children. They were not shamed in our presence because of their disability. Instead, they were touched. Seen. We listened to their stories. I saw many of the women weep, wiping away heartfelt tears with their chadars, overwhelmed with gratitude.

~

At one point, we had a free day and made the most of it. Doing the touristy thing, we went shopping on Chicken Street, which seems to have earned its name because a chicken shop was located on a corner during the early twentieth century. Several widows and children followed us begging for money. One little boy, in particular, was quite persistent. I finally just said, "I don't understand" in Dari. He immediately said in English, "Pay me to be your bodyguard!"

It wasn't easy getting around. There were steps into each store, tight quarters inside, and an uneven "sidewalk" that was riddled with cracks and potholes. But I loved the beautiful jewelry, handmade rugs, colorful scarves, and the bartering. One store displayed boxes made from the semiprecious stone, lapis lazuli. Several people were buying items, but I was just looking. With a typical sales pitch, the owner said to me, "Here, I will give you a gift," and set a bright blue lapis box on the counter.

"What are you doing in Afghanistan in a wheelchair?" he asked in English.

"We're giving wheelchairs to people with disabilities."

The store owner thanked us for what we were doing. We chatted a bit more, and, like a good tourist, I bought several lapis and wooden boxes.

As we were leaving, the man said, "I will be praying for you," his voice thick with emotion. I stopped and pushed my chair around.

"My son has polio and now lives in New York," he said. "Thank you for coming to help my people. I will be praying for your health."

The previous Friday, I had been too sick to attend church. Services were on Fridays in Afghanistan, not Sundays, following the customary workweek of Sunday through Thursday. In 2003, there was one Christian church that expatriates—and only expatriates—could legally attend. I've been told that by law the windows had to be closed when people sang worship music, but the windows could be opened once the sermon began. The service began at about two in the afternoon. Our team had arrived a bit late, so I squeezed inside the doors and immediately felt the hot, stale air in the building. I chose an empty spot in the back of the building near the windows and let my chadar fall off my head.

I heard multiple languages spoken, and it seemed every tribe, tongue, and nation (Rev. 7:9 NIV) was represented—except the Afghans who, of course, were not allowed by Afghan law in the building. We sang worship songs I knew, and a Frenchman gave the sermon in English. I'd forgotten to take medicine for my congestion, and I was miserable and overheated throughout the service. But it's an opportunity I am glad I didn't miss. In 2010, the church lost a legal battle concerning its lease, and the building was demolished. There's no longer a legal church building, even for expatriates, in Afghanistan.

A friend from Louisville worked for an NGO in Kabul. While I was planning my first trip, I asked Tracee if she knew a woman who would be willing to assist me while I was in the country. Within a few days of arriving in Kabul, Tracee introduced me to sixteen-year-old Nooria, who had a brother with a disability and was familiar with assisting him with his daily needs. I was hesitant to have a girl so young helping me, but my friends told me it would be a blessing to her family.

Tracee introduced me to Nooria and her mother at the guesthouse. While Nooria looked her age, her mother's tough life appeared in every wrinkle of her aged face. They were from the largest ethnic minority group in Afghanistan, the Hazara, thought to be the descendants of Genghis Khan.

After some discussion between my friends and Nooria and her mother, a salary was agreed upon: two dollars per hour, a rather large sum for an Afghan family. Nooria came in the mornings to help me get ready since I didn't have access to a bathroom. She'd often stay with us throughout the day, even going to the distributions. A few days into the trip, she saw that my hands were covered in dust and dirt from pushing my chair. She asked if I wanted my hands washed. I knew I had found a gem.

Although she spoke some English, when we first met, it was hard to know how much she understood since she was so reserved. I soon nicknamed her "the Little Rebel" after I watched her knowingly break the cultural norms and expose much more than was culturally appropriate. Rather than having long hair pulled back and hidden beneath a head covering, Nooria's black hair was cut bluntly at chin level. Oftentimes, I saw older Afghan women nudge her when she had allowed her chadar to slip off her head, revealing her hair.

Toward the end of my visit on a free day, I visited Nooria's house and met her family. The small mud-brick home had little to offer as far as comfort, especially with a large extended family living together. The interior was decorated simply with white-washed walls and a thin carpet of deep red. *Toshaks*, the traditional cushions used for seating guests and for sleeping, lined the walls around the room.

Nooria's brother, Mahram, was severely disabled since birth and could use only one hand. Although he had a wheelchair, I could see it was ill-fitting and falling to pieces. He sat on his twisted right leg, with his left leg strapped to the frame of the chair to prevent his foot from getting caught in the front casters. During our conversation, which unfolded in bits and pieces of English and Dari, Mahram told me that he often was depressed. I couldn't imagine how much his disability restricted his life. Even with a wheelchair, where could he go? Accessibility was nonexistent; it took several people to get me and my light-weight chair in and out of the guesthouse, transportation, and stores. Social stigma and shame restricted people with disabilities to begging or being hidden away in their homes.

Practicing traditional Afghan hospitality, Nooria served me juice in a small cardboard box with a straw. As she handed me the juice, my hands squeezed it a bit too tightly.

"Oh, I'm sorry," I gasped, as juiced spurted through the straw.

"Let me pour the juice into a cup," she offered.

Taking a dry glass, she grabbed an old plastic bottle filled with dirty water and poured it into the glass to clean it. Then she emptied the contents of the juice box into the wet glass. With a satisfied look on her face, she handed me the glass of juice.

This presented a dilemma. I knew the water had not come from a clean source. Do I risk having stomach problems, or do I offend this family by refusing their generosity? Fear won out, and as we continued to chat, I simply held the glass and didn't sip the juice. I still question the decision I made that day.

While I was at their house, I took Mahram's measurements for a new wheelchair. Thankfully, after I left, Lisa, Jeff, and Steve gave him a new chair that fit him properly.

~

I was both sad and glad to leave Afghanistan. It had been difficult. I couldn't get into any bathroom—not to wash my face or hands from the layers of dust, not to brush my teeth. I relied on Nooria and Lisa to rinse the cup I spit into after brushing my teeth, bring me a wet washcloth for my face each night, and empty the Sprite bottle full of pee.

Wearing the chadar was stifling and hot. It also took talent I didn't possess. The head covering constantly slipped off my head at first. After a few more trips to Afghanistan, I managed to get the hang of it, but I never grew fond of it (except on bad hair days or when it was really cold).

Then there's the culture. Although there are some lovely aspects of Afghan culture, such as its hospitality, the status of women was difficult for me to accept. During the first few trips, I had the opportunity to roll along the street, but only in the company of a male companion. In later years, security concerns prevented us from even leaving our accommodations.

One of the more difficult cultural norms for me was not making eye contact with men. I broke the no-eye-contact rule frequently when I noticed people staring at me. If it was a man, I would briefly make eye contact, nod, then slowly set my sight back down on the street in front of me. It was important to humanize myself. Oftentimes, men would nod in return and place their right hand over their heart, a common greeting in

Afghanistan. When I heard the "tsk, tsk, tsk" of a woman pitying me, I would make sure to greet her with a smile and say "*Salaam alaikum,*" a common greeting meaning "Peace be upon you."

Despite these hardships, I was willing to return.

People asked me, "Why Afghanistan?" My only answer was that you have to be crazy or called. Or maybe a bit of both. I truly felt God was leading me to Afghanistan. For what purpose, I was unsure. But I had been willing to go. And I was willing to return.

CHAPTER NINETEEN

I n the fall of 2004, Amelia and I flew through London again on our way to Afghanistan. We stayed with a family I'd met on a previous return flight from Dubai. They took us for lunch, and I opened the menu, attempting to decipher the options for food and drink. After the long flight, I was ready for a large drink to quench my thirst. I saw that the restaurant had apple cider and decided to order it. When the pint of cider arrived, I lifted the large mug for a sip and wrinkled my nose.

"Oh, this is beer!" I'd never been one who enjoyed beer or other alcoholic beverages.

"No, that's cider. That's just what it tastes like here," Rob said.

Not wanting to offend, I sipped the cider throughout the meal in an attempt to get rehydrated.

After returning to the house, Amelia asked, "Hey, want to take the train into London for a few hours?"

"I don't think I'm up to it. I feel . . . strange. I never get jet-lagged, but I guess this is what it feels like."

I opted to stay at the house and rest.

Later that evening over curry, the apple cider came up in a conversation. That's when my naivete was exposed. In England, cider is hard.

I hadn't been jet-lagged. I'd been tipsy!

The sports camp in Kabul that fall started off a bit rough. During the first week, Steve, Lisa, and I spoke with the man we'd met previously who was in charge of adaptive sports in Kabul. He was a double amputee and could easily push his chair, but his "assistant" pushed him as he talked on his phone and did everything at his beck and call. We nicknamed him "King Cripple." He said he knew nothing about the camp. On top of that, it was Ramadan. Lisa and I had planned the camp with King Cripple seven months earlier when we were in Afghanistan but hadn't checked the calendar to see when Ramadan would fall. After Lisa explained that several volunteers were on their way to help with the camp, he said, "You are our guests. We will have the camp."

A few days later, he showed up at the house with a request and played his final hand.

Through an interpreter, he said to me, "You can have the camp if I get a new wheelchair."

Bribery. It's very common in Afghanistan. I felt a rush of anger knowing this man drove his own car, had a personal assistant, and was sitting in a perfectly good wheelchair.

I took a deep, nervous breath and said, "*Nay.*" No.

Unfortunately, I didn't stop there. My frustration got the best of me.

"Can you translate this for me?" I asked Khushdel, an Afghan who worked for the organization.

"Why do you need a new chair when you don't even push the one you have by yourself?"

He left angry, without saying a word, and I realized what a terrible cultural faux pas I had just made. I had shamed an Afghan man.

Afghan culture, as most cultures of the Eastern world, is based on shame and honor. In the West, we think in terms of innocence and guilt that is individualistic. But the concept of honor and shame in the East is communal; shame on one person reflects shame on the entire family or community. As Westerners, we typically give direct yes or no answers. But honor-shame cultures characteristically speak indirectly, always wanting to save face.

Thankfully, despite my blunder, we were given access to the stadium. And King Cripple always pushed his chair in my presence after that day.

A number of volunteers, including Bree, were in Kabul. The coaches and wheelchair users who helped with the sports camp included Richard, our sports director; Mike, wheelchair tennis and rugby coach at the University of Arizona; and Danny, a lawyer and writer.

Staying in a rented house, we built a ramp, and I had access to a sink and toilet. What extravagance! During one day of distribution at Maiwand Hospital with the Afghan government's Ministry of the Disabled, several US military personnel joined us. Then we started the three-day sports clinic.

The camp was held at Ghazi Stadium, which was where the Taliban had enforced punishment under Sharia law. They dismembered, stoned, hanged, and shot people for crimes that included stealing, committing adultery, or murder. Thousands of people would pack the stands and watch as the grass of the soccer field became blood-soaked. Knowing the history of the stadium, it felt as if we were in the shadows of these ghosts as we encouraged men and women to enjoy the day while playing sports.

About twenty participants showed up for the camp. We separated into groups of men and women. Although I was dressed in long pants and a long-sleeved T-shirt with a chadar covering my head, I wished I had worn a shalwar chemise. My body felt exposed without the shalwar chemise, especially as I jumped in and played basketball with the men.

It didn't take long to see that the politics of a nation can be displayed in how a group plays team sports. Basketball was complete chaos at the beginning. After a while, we somewhat successfully imparted the concept of teamwork and cooperation. I was shocked when the men even began passing the ball to me. *That* is the power of sports.

The sports camp drew only a handful of women, but I was glad they had come. A massive billboard with Ahmad Shah Masoud, the celebrated mujahideen leader, overlooked the stadium as Mike coached the group of five women learning to play wheelchair tennis and basketball. Four of the women sat in sports wheelchairs wearing chadars as they played tennis with the rackets we brought. The other woman showed up in her blue burqa and didn't take it off. Somehow, she managed to hit the tennis balls over the net while looking through the blue woven material that covered her face, including her eyes.

Overall, the camp was a success. On the trip home, several of us traveled through Dubai and went out for dinner and walked along the city's waterway called the Creek. Two of the guys ordered a fruit-flavored hookah for kicks. Yes, I took a puff, which was more than enough to send me into a coughing fit.

During our time in Dubai, I felt my chair wobble as I pushed, but I brushed it off. As we returned to the hotel, we crossed a street and Bree helped me up the curb since the city didn't have many ramps. As I started pushing on the sidewalk, I heard, *ping!*

I squeezed both wrists against the push rims to stop my chair from rolling and looked down at my left wheel; a metal wire hung from the hub of my wheel.

"Agh, I have a broken spoke!"

Mike pushed over and took a look. "Aw, you'll be fine as long as you don't break more than a few."

Ping, ping, ping, ping, ping, ping, ping.

"Well, that's unfortunate," he said.

While we made our way back to the hotel, I sauntered behind everyone, hoping the wheel would sustain my weight with half the spokes flopping from the hub as the wheel rotated, sounding like a discordant windchime.

Once I was in my hotel room, the guys swapped the twenty-five-inch wheels from my tennis chair—made of light-weight carbon fiber spokes—for the twenty-four-inch wheels with metal spokes and solid tires I used to avoid flats. We didn't take the time to adjust the brakes, so Bree held the chair in place while I transferred into bed that night.

On our layover in Paris the next day, we took a few hours to go sightseeing. With each push, my chair pulled to the right and became more difficult to move. I finally stopped and looked down. The right tire was flat. This was one of those times you don't dare ask, "What else could go wrong?"

I didn't have an extra tube in my carry-on luggage since I normally used solid tires. So we did the only thing possible: on the right side, we placed my everyday chair's 24-inch wheel, and on my left, the 25-inch sports wheel. I sat unevenly in my chair and probably looked as if I'd had a bit too much cider again as I pushed in a crooked, crisscrossed pattern through the Paris, Atlanta, and Louisville airports.

Accidentally tipsy from hard apple cider, puffing on a hookah, and pushing a lopsided wheelchair through three airports all on the same trip. These are the stories that get left out of newsletters to financial and prayer supporters.

CHAPTER TWENTY

B efore my first trip to Afghanistan, I drove downtown to Louisville's main library. While scouring the languages section, I found a beginner's book on Farsi. Farsi is spoken in Iran, while Dari is the dialect in Afghanistan. Both are considered Persian; it's similar to the differences in American English and British English. This small book was the best I could find since the internet hadn't yet exploded with language programs. I started learning the Arabic script and memorized some useful vocabulary. That book traveled with me all the way to Afghanistan on my first trip. Nooria helped me with pronunciation and grammar. Upon my return to the US, I looked for new resources and continued to soak in the language of many of the Afghan people. On return visits to Afghanistan, I was able to carry on brief conversations, but I wanted to connect at a heart level with the people of Afghanistan. Using an interpreter is so formal and prevented me from truly communicating on a deeper level.

A blonde, blue-eyed, wheelchair-using American woman is the last person anyone in any country expects to speak their language. On a later trip, Miriam and I—both with visible disabilities—waited in line for immigration at the airport in Kabul. We were pulled aside while others were allowed to continue through the line. Behind me, I heard a guard say in Dari, "She's sick."

Oh, buddy. Exhausted after two days of travel, I turned around quickly and irritably replied in Dari, "I am *not* sick."

The guards' eyes bugged out, and they quickly escorted us through immigration and customs.

Of course, there also is miscommunication. While interviewing a woman at a distribution, I asked how she had become disabled. I was certain I misunderstood her. *What could a cow have to do with becoming disabled?*

When I asked an interpreter to assist, he explained, "She was gored by a bull."

Well, at least I hadn't completely misunderstood.

Despite gaping holes in my ability to speak Dari, a little bit goes a long way when I showed a true interest in learning the language and culture. Speaking from my heart to another person in their language was a precious gift to both of us.

It was this desire to speak heart-to-heart in Dari that took me down a surprising road and indirectly led to a giant leap in my independence.

I began searching for language programs. Ideally, I wanted to go to language school in Kabul, but I knew that would be difficult physically, so I looked for programs in the United States. As I scoured the internet, I stumbled across classes in the Department of Middle Eastern Studies at the University of Arizona. The university offered Persian classes with an emphasis on Farsi, the Iranian dialect. It just seemed like a pipe dream, not something I would actually get to do. I couldn't imagine moving out of state without my support system. But three days later I received a call.

I'd first met Mike in Mazatlán, then he gave me the push to transfer by myself at the Tucson tennis tournament before coaching at the camp in Kabul. For the past several years, he'd been trying to convince me to come to the University of Arizona to play tennis.

"Hello, Jennifer Lynn," he said.

I laughed. "Hey, Mike."

He started his typical spiel. "Come out to Arizona. Play tennis with us and attend school out here."

My typical response was "I don't need another degree." But that day my worlds collided. He was asking me to play tennis for and attend the very university I had just discovered offered Persian classes.

This time I said, "I'm listening."

In August 2005, I moved into the graduate dorms at the University of Arizona. I was thirty-two, and it was my first time living away from home. My parents thought I was nuts. I just kept reminding them, "I could be in Kabul, you know." That always shut them down fairly quickly.

Before going to Arizona, I was still living at home, although it wasn't because my parents had been overprotective. The reason I lived at home was one of convenience. The addition to our house provided the best accessible accommodations I could ever want—or afford. Why did I need to move out? Once I was traveling an average of ten weeks a year, it gave me a break from my parents, and my parents had a break from me too.

Several factors made moving to Arizona for two semesters a bit easier. Thankfully, my financial supporters contributed enough money for the two classes and rent since the classes were job-related. Already knowing several people in Tucson was helpful too. Mike worked at the university, and Bree was an undergraduate student. On top of that, I had family—aunts, an uncle, and cousins—just two hours away in the Phoenix area, and I was excited to get to visit them on occasion. I felt as if I had a safety net around me in case something unexpected happened.

While I continued working for the Mobility Project about thirty hours a week, I added learning a new language to my list of responsibilities. Knowing that a classroom setting is not ideal for language learning, I made myself speak in class as often as possible to get used to making the embarrassing mistakes that are part of the process.

During the first week of class, my professor asked me a question in Persian. I nervously responded with the vocabulary and accent that I used in Afghanistan.

"You sound just like them!" he responded. "Them" meaning Afghans; my professor was of Iranian descent.

Thank you. I'll take that as a compliment!

At least he didn't say I sounded like a Kentuckian speaking Persian.

Because of the heat, tennis practice was scheduled at a staggering six in the morning three or four days a week. Since I need a good eight hours of sleep at minimum, not only were the early mornings a challenge, but I also had to plan my gimpy life around this schedule. How would I make time to have help taking a shower? To do the bowel program?

I found a grad student to help with personal care. Heather was getting her master's in physiological sciences, and we worked great together throughout my time in Arizona. She came three mornings and three evenings a week; the other days I did everything on my own. The bigger concern was how to pay for the help I needed.

Personal care—dressing, showering, assistance with bladder and bowel care, preparing meals, and household work, such as laundry—is not covered by private health insurance. When I was injured, I'd qualified for Medicaid as a secondary insurance since I was disabled as a minor. Medicaid paid for personal care services, but once I started teaching ESL part-time, I lost those benefits because I made more than I was allowed to by government standards.

Thankfully, I finally qualified for a state program that allowed me to hire caregivers and pay for their services; it had taken more than eight years on the waiting list before I received services through this program. In my experience, the lack of options to pay for personal care is the single largest barrier to employment and living independently for people with disabilities. If you make money, you are often punished by losing the very services that allow you to work.

With a caregiver to help me several times a week, I had my personal care needs covered. The dorm's accessible kitchen and washer and dryer allowed me to cook my meals and do laundry. Little by little, I discovered that living independently was possible.

My goal at the university was to study, but not to be the overachieving perfectionist I'd always been. I was mildly successful. I did well in both of my classes without overstudying or getting stressed about tests. Tennis on the other hand . . .

I'd been playing tennis for about four years when I went to the University of Arizona, but I was never what I consider a good player. Tennis was a challenge, a good workout, and a stress reliever. I wasn't out to win tournaments. But even with the increased practice schedule, great coaching, and teammates, I still don't remember winning a single match during a tournament that year. By the end of the season, I ended one practice in tears from the frustration of not winning a single game in a match against a teammate.

Learning Persian was my primary reason for going to Arizona. Getting to play tennis was a bonus. What I didn't know, but see clearly now, was that my real reason to be there was I needed a good strong push to get me on my own two feet . . . or wheels.

CHAPTER TWENTY-ONE

During the spring of 2006, my grandma joined me on a distribution in Costa Rica. Even at eighty-two, she was up for adventure.

During the wheelchair distributions, she helped with administration. However, Grandma was more comfortable making small talk with the team members. With her sense of humor and zest for life, she'd earned the title "World's Coolest Grandma" before the most memorable part of the trip.

On our free day, the group of staff and volunteers took the opportunity to explore the gorgeous scenery of Costa Rica. Beginning on a bus tour that took us to a coffee plantation, we saw ancient, gnarled trees, as well as acres and acres of coffee trees. I pushed along an easily accessible path with my grandma at my side as magnificent waterfalls thundered into the river below us.

But the highlight of our day was the canopy tour. The canopy is the densely foliaged area of the rain forest. The tour took us treetop to treetop via zip lines. Both my grandma and I jumped at the once-in-a-lifetime opportunity.

Our group included twelve able-bodied staff and volunteers and three chair users. In harnesses and bright yellow helmets, our group waited on a wooden platform that overlooked a valley full of lush green trees, vines, and dense vegetation. The sun was shining bright, yet it was comfortably cool in the mountains.

Grandma and I chose to have park employees—who just happened to be handsome, young Costa Rican men—ride tandem with us; they would access the hand brake to slow us down as we approached each platform. I asked to have my chair with me on each platform so I could sit comfortably and protect my bottom. An employee zipped himself and my chair to the first platform as my tandem partner hung beside me, both of us swinging under the thick cable. Before our first run, I took a little time to figure out how to keep my balance. I wrapped my right arm around his neck, and my legs were supported by his, almost like I was sitting sideways in his lap.

He looked at me. "*Lista?*" Ready?

I nodded.

We glided across the zip line, and I soaked in the breath-taking beauty of the plants, tropical birds, and animals inhabiting the canopy as we soared high above the rain forest. As we neared the platform, ninety or so feet above the ground, my tandem buddy applied the hand brake and brought us to a stop at the platform. He handed me off to another park employee who placed me in my chair and moved the carabiners from one zip line to the next. The other chair users, Rich and Danny, opted to sit on small buckets. Midway through the tour, a downpour fit for a rain forest moved through, leaving my orange tank top rain-soaked. Between two platforms, we traveled along a trail that was too steep and rough for my chair. I was carried over-the-threshold-style by several of the park employees for a few hundred feet before they passed me off to the next worker, while Rich and Danny were piggybacked to the next platform. The last of the nine zip lines took us over a river rushing with white rapids.

The beauty and adventure of the day were amazing, but hearing my grandma's enthusiastic laugh and whoop of excitement reverberate through the rain forest as she soared through the trees is what I treasure most.

When someone asks me where I get the courage to try the impossible, I smile and tell them, "I had the World's Coolest Grandma."

Not all trips go as planned. Later that year, I helped with the summer groups in Mexico for several weeks and returned in December for the sports camp. Richard planned a tennis tournament for the weekend after the camps in Mazatlán and Culiacán.

After the two camps concluded, I hit some tennis balls on the court to get ready for the tournament and noticed that my spasticity was pretty bad. Since I had received the baclofen pump fourteen years earlier, my spasms only caused me problems on rare occasions. I simply thought I might have a UTI, which could increase my spasticity, and decided to wait until morning to see how I felt.

By two in the morning, my spasms were so bad that my entire body was convulsing, and I was also slightly feverish. I realized that my pump wasn't functioning correctly. I was going into withdrawal from the medication, which can be deadly.

I called my doctor's office, but the answering service didn't pick up. So I tried calling Medtronic, the manufacturer of the pump, but with no luck. As a last resort, I called Dr. Shaw's home number, not wanting to wake him at five o'clock in the morning.

He answered. I explained the situation and asked, "What should I do?"

"Try heading to the ER while I get some more information. When is your next alarm date?"

"My next refill is on Tuesday, but my alarm date isn't for another two weeks."

Every few months, a doctor needed to refill the pump with medication. If the medication got too low, an alarm inside the pump would beep, indicating the pump needed to be filled.

"I'll see what I can find out, while you head to the ER."

I hung up the phone, then called loudly to wake up the person sleeping in the room next to me.

"Can you wake up Jeff or Brock and see if one of them can take me to the hospital?"

After Lisa helped me dress and transfer into my chair, she pushed me down to the parking lot, and Brock lifted me into the front seat of the van. I felt like I was on a bucking bronco. My body was contracting every three seconds, a painful contortion of muscles pulling me forward and knocking the breath out of me, then tossing me backward against the seat. Every bump in the road set off more spasms during the twenty-minute trip.

At the emergency room in Mazatlán, I explained that I needed to speak with a neurosurgeon, figuring he or she would know if Medtronic equipment was available in the city and possibly have access to the small device that could read the computer chip in my pump. In the room, Hazuki, Rich's wife, waited with me.

A doctor came in, and I explained the situation. Speaking in

Spanish with a neurosurgeon while in withdrawal is a true accomplishment, in my opinion. Thankfully, Hazuki was fluent in Spanish and assisted when necessary. The doctor was familiar with Medtronic, but only for its cardiac products. Just then, my phone rang; it was Dr. Shaw. I apologized to the doctor and answered the phone.

"Medtronic found that the batteries in the pumps made when yours was are defective," he told me after I explained my situation. "The pump slows down near the refill date. That's why you're not getting enough medicine. Jenny, you need to get on the first flight back to the US."

It was nine thirty when we left the hospital. On the ride back to the hotel, I arranged for a flight to Louisville that morning. I always travel with what-if situations in mind and had oral baclofen with me. I began taking the prescribed dose to offset the withdrawal, but it didn't help much.

Unfortunately, I'd been through withdrawal once before when the surgeon and I waited too long to replace my first pump and the battery died. Fortunately, I knew what to do and how to prepare the people around me.

After I returned to the hotel, Kerry, a volunteer, helped me pack.

"When I take medicine, I need to write it down. One of the side effects of withdrawal is short-term memory loss, so I might start forgetting things," I explained. "Can you start making sure that I record when I take the baclofen?"

Despite my protests that I'd be fine on the trip home, my friends and coworkers were worried about me flying back on my own. Brock offered to fly home with me. It was a good thing he did.

In Houston, I vaguely remember waiting sleepily in line to board the plane for my connecting flight, my head resting on the carry-on that was on my lap. I don't have any recollection of the flight to Louisville. Brock later told me I was unconscious. He had to hold me upright while the plane was landing so I wouldn't fall forward. Getting off the plane, I briefly saw my dad as an airport employee and Brock picked me up like a ragdoll and placed me in the aisle chair to exit the plane.

My dad drove me straight to Dr. Stevens's office; he was waiting for me. The only thing I remember was hearing him say, "Jenny, I'm so sorry you are going through this."

Confused and disoriented, I woke up the next morning in my bed. After summoning up the memories of the pump malfunctioning in Mexico and flying home, I lifted the covers to see what I was wearing. Same clothes. My body was calm, and I could move without setting off spasms. Just then my mom opened the door quietly and peeked in my room.

"I'm awake."

My parents were leaving for a trip to Nebraska, so my grandma was grateful when Brock offered to stay an extra day or two; they had become buddies on our Costa Rica trip and zip-lining adventure.

A bit later, I called Leslie to update her on the situation.

"Are you drunk?" she finally asked, laughing.

No, but I was evidently *very* happy to have had a friend—whom I had a crush on—travel home with me. Leslie will never let me live down that conversation, especially since, according to her, I was talking so loudly that everyone in the house—Brock included—had to have heard every word I said.

It was a good thing he stayed. The next day I recognized that I was hallucinating when "memories" weren't making sense, which is another sign of withdrawal. I returned to the hospital, and Dr. Stevens admitted me for observation.

A psychiatrist gave me a mental status exam; I have no clue

if I passed it. My short-term memory was definitely affected. I remember Brock making a checklist on the whiteboard in the hospital room. Every time I repeated a question, he put a checkmark next to the topic. There were a lot of check marks. In a state of confusion and with no filter on my mouth, I asked him, "Have I taken my birth control pills?"

Oh, the embarrassment. Some things I wish I didn't remember.

Thankfully, the doctors decided I was experiencing the latent effects of withdrawal and the pump was working fine.

I can read your thoughts: "What happened to the guy you had a crush on?" Well, it didn't go anywhere. But let's get sidetracked for a moment and talk about sex and sexuality after a spinal cord injury.

My single able-bodied girlfriends often complain about people (like nosy church ladies or concerned parents) constantly asking if they're dating anyone. My friends despise this question. But I've been asked it only a handful of times, and I'm taken aback when it happens. I've even thanked the person for asking.

Why? Because they see past my wheelchair. They see me, a woman. A woman who happens to use a wheelchair who enjoys a little eye candy. Who sighs at the thought of a Mr. Knightley by my side. A woman who wants to look and feel desirable.

Picture in your mind what a woman using a wheelchair looks like. What do you see? By and large, our society strips away a person's sexuality when they have a disability. Men deal with this just as much, if not more, than women.

When my photo ran in an article in *USA Today*, a reader

commented: "She can't be disabled. She's too pretty to be in a wheelchair."

Huh? If we follow this logic, we're led to the false conclusion that disability and attractiveness, specifically sexual attractiveness, are mutually exclusive. Allow me to let you in on a not-so-little secret: sexuality and disability can—and do—coexist. People with disabilities come in all shapes, sizes, and colors. Just like the able-bodied population.

When I first met Terri, I was surprised by her style and confidence. Leslie at the Ms. Wheelchair America pageant didn't conform to my image of a quadriplegic. She was independent, stunning, and . . . *married*. I had fallen for this misconception without even knowing it until the "roll models" in my life challenged my stereotypes, including the beliefs I unconsciously held about myself.

Whether or not it makes you uncomfortable, people with disabilities are sexual beings. If your daughter or son was just diagnosed with a spinal cord injury, they're still a teenager with hormones. They still want to feel attractive. Your daughter still can become pregnant. Your son will continue to want girls to "like" him. Well, let's be honest. He has more on his mind than girls just liking him.

For the man who was recently disabled, it's in his thoughts. Will he ever be "man" enough for his wife? A woman may wonder if her significant other will still love her. Both are questioning their value and sexual attractiveness in a new body.

While we're on the topic, let's talk about sex (because I know you're thinking about it). Yes, women and men with spinal cord injuries can have sex. Female anatomy doesn't change after an injury. Women continue to have their period, although spinal shock may halt it for up to a year. (That may be the only upside of a spinal cord injury, and I didn't get this bonus.) Women with spinal cord injuries can become pregnant and have a family. There's also research that shows women with spinal cord injuries can orgasm just as frequently as able-bodied women because the vagus nerve, which is a neural pathway for sexual stimulation, runs outside the spinal cord.

For men with spinal cord injuries, sex is a bit more complicated. Typically, pharmaceutical intervention is needed to maintain or sustain an erection or ejaculation. Retrograde ejaculation, where semen backs up into the bladder, or a complete lack of ejaculation are common challenges, which make fathering a child more difficult, or sometimes impossible, without medical intervention.

For both women and men, it's common for there to be heightened sensation above the level of injury during sex. Some people even reach orgasm just from stimulation above their level of injury.

With all that being said, there are challenges to consider for relationships and sex when a spinal cord injury is added to the mix, but that's true of any relationship, wheelchair or not. I have many friends with disabilities who are wonderful spouses and parents. And *that* is what's important.

Whew. I think that's enough sex talk for now.

My Mr. Knightley—or Mr. Darcy, if he were interested— hasn't come my way yet. One thing God has shown me is *anything* is possible. Oh, Lord, have mercy on that man.

CHAPTER TWENTY-TWO

Within the first two months of living independently in Arizona, I decided I didn't ever want to move back in with my parents. At age thirty-three, I'd finally discovered that with an accessible kitchen and appliances and hiring a personal care attendant several times a week, I could handle life on my own. No offense, Mom and Dad, but I was finally ready to fly the coop.

As my time in Arizona came to a close in 2006, I began looking for a place to live in Louisville.

But where? The most obvious choice was an apartment. However, the word "accessible" has many meanings. Not one of the "accessible" apartments on the market fit my needs. So I began to research buying a house I could modify. That proved too expensive because the modifications would include remodeling a kitchen, master bath, and entrances.

Finally, I settled on buying a condo in a new development where construction hadn't begun. I could make a few changes to the floor plan and avoid the cost of after-the-fact modifications. In addition, the homeowners association would be responsible for maintaining the exterior of the building, including yard work and snow removal.

With the help of Leslie's husband, who was a real estate agent, I found a two-bedroom condominium with an open floor plan. The developer was willing to make changes in the kitchen and master bathroom without an upcharge. My modifications included a roll-in shower, sinks in the kitchen and bathroom that I could roll under, an oven relocated next to the sink and with the controls on the front panel, and thirty-four-inch-high countertops (two inches lower than the normal height). The laundry room, closet, and bathroom doors were changed to pocket doors to allow room for maneuverability.

Then the fun began: decorating. After hours and hours of watching home remodeling shows, I was ready to choose paint colors, flooring, cabinets, and furniture. My penny-pinching skills came in handy as I purchased a kitchen table and six chairs at an antique mall. I waited and waited for the price to drop on a couch; I eventually bought the floor model. The finishing touches included pottery from Afghanistan, family heirlooms, as well as Craigslist purchases. I created my own home-sweet-accessible home.

I also chose to look for a roommate, more for safety than companionship since I still had a fear of falling or something going badly. A friend connected me with Emily who was moving to Louisville for a job with a nonprofit organization. We finalized the arrangements, and Emily moved in a week before me. While I was in Costa Rica for work, my parents moved my clothing into the condo. Upon my return, I moved my remaining belongings into my new home.

I enjoyed the camaraderie of a roommate: sharing cooking and cleanup in the kitchen, watching movies together. I tried to make sure Emily was always "just" a roommate and never a caregiver. There were times I asked for help, but I wanted to make sure I didn't take advantage of her and place her in a role for which she didn't sign up. When she moved out to get married two years later, I decided to try living on my own. I have loved the freedom.

Having my own place was another step toward independence.

Merriam-Webster's definition of independence is the quality or state of not being under the control of, reliant on, or connected with someone or something else.

Yes, I rely on a caregiver for some personal care and housekeeping. I would change it if I could in a heartbeat. I hate having to plan my life around someone else's schedule.

But when I'm asked if I live independently, I answer yes. I live in my condo. I work, drive, visit with friends and family, play sports, and live a mostly normal life. I view it as the classic example of seeing the glass half empty or half full. I choose to see the independence I've gained instead of dwelling on what I can't do on my own.

But it can be exhausting.

On the mornings when I have no help, it's a workout just to get dressed. I wake to the sound of my alarm clock, reach over, and tap it to turn it off. I slide a dimmer switch attached to my nightstand to turn on a floor lamp. I hook my left wrist under the push rim of my manual chair at the side of my bed, and I use my bicep to pull my upper body so I can prop up on my elbow. I roll the blankets down so I can see my legs. I use momentum to rock back and forth and swing my hands behind me so I can sit up. Since I sleep on my side with my legs bent, I use my wrists and arms to move my lifeless legs into a straight position. If I get light-headed because of low blood pressure, I lie back down before I continue. I catheterize and ensure my backside is good to go by turning on my right side and looking in a mirror.

I begin dressing myself in the clothes I laid out the previous night. Grabbing them, I put each leg through my underwear and tug them up with my thumb or wrist, rolling side to side. I repeat that process with my pants. One at a time, I pull a leg up and cross it over the other to scoot my socks and shoes onto each of my feet. My shoes always slip on with stretchy laces, or fasten with zippers or Velcro, so I don't have to tie laces.

To get into my chair, I lift my body with my arms to scoot to the side of the bed, being careful not to lose my balance. I move one leg at a time over the edge of the bed until both legs sit on the footrest of my chair. I grab the sliding board and scoot it under my bottom. In one swift movement, I lift and scoot myself over the sliding board into my chair.

On the three mornings I have help, my personal care attendant arrives at seven o'clock. I transfer with help into a rolling shower chair since bare butts don't slide. After a quick shower, my PCA transfers me back into bed and puts on my underwear, pants, socks, and shoes. If I have any worrisome red spots on my rear, I have an extra set of eyes to check my skin.

Once I'm in my chair, I dress my top half, blow dry my hair, and put on my makeup while my aide gets lunch ready for me to take to work, takes out the trash, folds laundry, and cleans the kitchen. By 8:45, I'm typically ready to head out the door to work.

Although I'm insanely envious of those who are completely independent of any assistance, the help I receive a few days a week saves me time and energy for other activities. In my situation, doing all that without help actually would leave me too exhausted for other things in life.

I choose to view independence on a continuum; some of us need more assistance in meeting our basic needs than others to live healthy and active lives. I don't believe independence is the absence of help or assistance. Aren't all humans—abled-bodied or disabled—dependent on each other? Maybe interdependent is a better word. We all need support and encouragement from others.

I am independent. I'm in charge of my daily routine, which includes accepting the help I need from others.

CHAPTER TWENTY-THREE

On February 6, 2007, I walked—or rolled—the catwalk during New York Fashion Week. My smile wasn't forced one bit while I paused for pictures on the red carpet, cameras flashing and reporters yelling for my attention. It was like living out a movie script from someone else's life.

This opportunity began in 2004 when I sent a video and essay to Discovery through Design, an organization searching for four "roll models." According to a press release, the roll models would help "banish stereotypes of women with disabilities; to celebrate the accomplishments of disabled women; to promote unbiased treatment; and to raise funds for women's health care initiatives and spinal cord injury research." The winners would also receive a new wheelchair and a paid trip to New York City.

It ended up being so much more than a new chair and a trip to New York.

~

Four incredible "chair-women" founded Discovery through Design and organized the Rolling with Style Gala. Marilyn Hamilton transformed the wheelchair industry after a hang gliding accident left her with a spinal cord injury in 1978. She took the technology used in hang gliding and created the first fashionable, ultra-lightweight wheelchairs and founded Quickie Wheelchairs. Wendy Crawford became a quadriplegic at nineteen when a drunk driver hit the vehicle in which she was a passenger; she was on her way to the airport to fly to Japan for her first international modeling contract. Julia Dorsett, a Paralympic athlete, and actress/restaurateur Ashley Lauren Fisher rounded out the four women with a vision and passion for women using wheelchairs.

Incredibly, I was one of the four roll models chosen for the Rolling with Style Gala at Cipriani 42nd Street, which was part fashion show, part fundraiser.

A fashion designer, who created a piece of custom clothing and a one-of-a-kind Quickie wheelchair, was assigned to each roll model and chairwoman. Designers included St. John, Kimora Lee Simmons, Nicole Miller, Zang Toi, Marc Bouwer, Lloyd Klein, and Thom Browne. And the event was inclusive: for each roll model, there were three able-bodied models.

The speaker for the event was Lesley Stahl of CBS's *60 Minutes*. The morning of the fashion show we were interviewed for a segment covering the gala. After the interview, it was time to get dolled up. The models dressed at the hotel, then crossed the street to the venue, where hairstylists curled my stick-straight hair in ways I didn't know were possible. My designer, Zang Toi, instructed the makeup artist to do dark, smoky eyes and a nude lip. It was gorgeous. More importantly, I felt gorgeous.

After hair and makeup, all the models gathered backstage

for rehearsal. The stage manager explained in what order we were going and told us where to stop at the end of the runway, how to pause and turn around. That sounded easy enough.

As the public entered for the reception, the roll models walked the red carpet in our designer clothes and new chairs, telling the reporters "who" we were wearing. Just before the event began, we lined up backstage, makeup artists touching up lipstick and powdering noses. That was when I realized they didn't tell us *how* to go down the runway. Should I simply smile or do I "smize" a la *America's Next Top Model?*

I decided this was New York Fashion Week, and I was going to play it like a real model. As I rolled up the ramp waiting for the previous model to exit the runway, I took a deep breath while my stomach fluttered with nerves.

I turned the corner and maneuvered my chair down the long, narrow walkway; cameras flashed, and the spotlights shined brightly in my eyes. While I tried to remember the things I'd learned in a modeling class, I heard the clicks of cameras and applause from the audience. *Don't look down. Look straight ahead.* I kept the serious model look on my face but caught myself nervously glancing down a few times to see where the runway ended. At the end of the runway, surrounded by guests and photographers, I turned my chair to a forty-five-degree angle and briefly paused, spun the chair to the left and paused, and turned around to roll back up the runway.

Turning the corner, Julia, who had been watching on the monitor, said to me, "You did the kickass walk!"

I laughed out loud. "Yes, I did."

I won't lie. I still struggle with my body image. I'll never be the picture-perfect model on the cover of *Vogue*. On most days, I have learned to accept myself as I am.

The movie *The Greatest Showman* is a fictional story of Phineas T. Barnum. However, it's the stars of the show with whom I resonate: Lettie (the bearded woman), Anne (a trapeze artist), Charles (the little person General Tom Thumb), and the other performers hired as "unique persons" for Barnum's show. It's the characters' ability to eventually embrace their differences that has me watching the movie over and over again.

After my injury, I felt like Lettie. I hid my atrophied legs and arms. I tried not to draw attention to my quadly hands. I was ashamed of my bladder and bowel dysfunction. These were my "broken parts," as Lettie puts it. I've spoken to enough people to know that I'm not alone in struggling with insecurities.

Barnum sees something special—something beautiful—in their physical differences. As Lettie stands behind a curtain away from the stares of the audience, Barnum tells her, "They don't know it yet, but they're going to love you." Often other people in our lives can see something in us that we can't see in ourselves. As I met women and men with spinal cord injuries, I slowly learned from them. I developed courage and confidence. I've honestly shared my struggles to encourage others.

Just as P.T.'s band of oddities found solace in each other's company, I've learned to make no apologies for who I am. Like Lettie, I can say, "This is me." Accepting my body is a proclamation to not be defined by the world's standards. To let go of what others think. Oh, the freedom that comes with acceptance.

∿

Nothing felt sexy about having a Foley catheter.

The catheter began slipping off the leg bag after I returned from Arizona. I'd look down and see my pants were wet where the bag was hidden inside my underwear. After seventeen years of having an indwelling catheter, I couldn't figure out why it was happening. Representatives from medical supply companies had no answers.

When I lived in Arizona, I met another female quad who was a graduate student. Katie had had a surgery that allowed her to independently catheterize. This procedure, called a Mitrofanoff, involved surgically creating a small catheterizable stoma—or a small hole—in her abdominal region and enlarged her bladder.

At the time, I didn't think there was a reason for me to consider this surgery. Yes, it would be nice to not have the bag and to have more options for clothing. But I was independent in the bladder regimen I had. I rarely had urinary tract infections, and I rarely had problems with leaking. Except for vanity's sake, why fix what wasn't broken?

But the frustration of the uncooperative catheters became an issue. And I must admit that the experience in New York, when I wore the beautiful dress with the leg bag strapped to my thigh, had impacted me too. When the bag was strapped to my leg, I couldn't reach it to empty it without help, and I was afraid it might show. What if I ever got married? Did I really want an indwelling catheter and leg bag around all the time?

I called Katie and asked about the surgery and her experience. I also spoke with several other people who'd had this procedure. Finally, it was time to get a professional opinion.

I made an appointment with a urologist in Louisville. When I asked about the surgery, he advised me to have the procedure. This shocked me since I had been thinking of it until then as a vanity surgery: elective and solely for looks. The urologist was the first person to explain there was an increased risk of bladder cancer with indwelling catheters.

Since there wasn't a urologist in Louisville who was trained to do this operation, I contacted the surgeon who had performed Katie's surgery and made an appointment with him to coincide with a trip I had already planned to Philadelphia in August 2007.

When we met, Dr. Shenot explained the procedure. In short, a section of small bowel tissue is used to increase the size of the bladder and create a stoma in my lower abdomen. He emphasized the benefits and recommended the surgery since I wasn't yet experiencing a damaged urethra, which causes the catheter to come out easily or urine to leak, and I wasn't showing signs of cancer. The goal for the surgery was to be able to hold 500 cc to 800 cc of urine, a little more than an average able-bodied person.

I gave myself several weeks to come to a decision. Was it worth the risk and possible complications? I waited until my self-imposed deadline to make the decision, then called and scheduled the surgery.

My mom and I arrived in Philadelphia in October 2007. My aunt, Jacquee, lived in the area, and we stayed at her house during my recovery. In addition, Katie, who was from the area, had a modified van she let us use during those five weeks.

During the surgery, the doctor put a nasogastric (NG) tube through my nose, down my throat and into my stomach to remove gas and fluids until my bowels began to move again, which could take up to ten days. The NG tube and not being allowed to eat were the worst parts of the first week.

Regulating the pain medication was difficult too. Although I couldn't feel the pain from the incision with thirty-seven staples, my body still recognized the discomfort of surgery. I experienced increased blood pressure, goose bumps, blurred vision, rapid heartbeat, and shaking. This phenomenon is called autonomic dysreflexia and occurs when people have spinal cord injuries at or above the sixth thoracic vertebra, meaning they're paralyzed from the chest down. I call autonomic dysreflexia "God's emergency backup system." These signs let me know when something is wrong below my level of injury. If left unchecked, the exceptionally high blood pressure from autonomic dysreflexia can cause a stroke, or in rare cases, death. Many health professionals are unfamiliar with AD, and those of us with spinal cord injuries often must educate doctors and nurses and advocate for ourselves.

I spent ten days in the hospital. Within four weeks of the surgery, I was catheterizing through the stoma, which was bright pink and as small as a pencil eraser. It was easy to insert the catheter into the stoma, but at first, sticking a foreign object into a hole in my body felt like a "Stupid Human Tricks" segment.

I returned home five weeks after surgery and settled back into my usual routine. My bladder easily holds 500 cc to 600 cc. I wake up once during the night to catheterize with a closed-system intermittent catheter—a disposable catheter and bag— that I empty the next morning.

Was it difficult? Yes.

Was it worth it? Yes.

After the surgery, I bought my first pair of Gap jeans that fit and some cute panties from Victoria's Secret.

CHAPTER TWENTY-FOUR

On a muggy Saturday morning, just before moving to Arizona, I arrived at the boathouse on the Ohio River already nervous at the thought of getting on the water. Randy Mills, the director of Louisville Adaptive Rowing, had pestered me until I gave in, saying, "Once. I'll try it once."

I approached the ramp that went down to the dock and paused. It was alarmingly steep.

"Can you stand behind me . . . just in case?" I asked Randy.

Once I safely descended the ramp and was on the dock, I took in the view. To my left were Louisville's downtown skyline and two bridges that cross the river to Indiana. Opposite the dock, about 150 feet away, was the densely forested Towhead Island, which created a narrow chute of water 800 meters long and protected the dock from the wakes created by the barges heading up or down the river. The chirping of birds, the buzzing of insects, a splash of a fish, and ducks paddling in the water acted as a welcoming committee.

Two volunteers lifted me out of my chair and into a beginner's boat for two people. My seat, in the stern of the boat, had a seat with a backrest and did not slide like the gliding seats for able-bodied rowers. Randy stepped into and sat in the bow seat. Donning a chest strap for balance, a life vest for safety, and gloves to keep the oars in my hands, we pushed away from the dock and floated into the narrow channel between the shoreline and island.

Randy sat behind me that first morning and explained the basics of rowing. First, you sit backward in the boat. My back faced the direction in which we were going to row. He explained how to drop the oars behind me in the water, pull the oars toward my chest, push down on the oar handles to pop the oars out of the water, then move the oars away from my body and drop them back in the water for the catch. Each step required concentration, and it felt like a complicated choreography of steps rather than one smooth, continuous movement of a single stroke.

After dropping the oars in the water and pulling through the stroke a few times, I got the hang of the basics of rowing. But it wasn't pretty. The oars wouldn't stay in the right position because of my lack of grip. I had to focus on my balance and compensate for the lack of function in my weaker right side.

With Coach Bob Hurley's ingenuity, we figured out how to fix the oarlocks so the oars would stay in the proper position. I rowed with the blades "squared" since I couldn't turn the oar handles, called feathering, as other rowers do.

The rhythm of the stroke, the sound of the water, and the surrounding nature were surprisingly calming.

Over the next several years, we continued to tweak the oars and the boat as my strength and technique improved. I started to row in a competitive shell, and Bob shortened a pair of lighter oars to match my short, fast stroke. I found new gloves that helped my hands grip the oars better. I stopped wearing the life vest that hindered my stroke and simply tossed one in the boat, a law when rowing or boating on the Ohio River.

When the boathouse got a single racing shell for para-rowers, I was ready. In the single, I was responsible for steering and looking behind me to ensure I was headed in the right direction.

Being out of my wheelchair provided a freedom of movement for which I was willing to get up at six on Saturday mornings. When I said "yes" to rowing, I didn't know it would turn into a love affair with being on the water.

I'm often questioned about rowing on the Ohio River.

"Yuck. Why would you want to row in the Ohio?" people ask, referring to its murky water, known for its pollution.

"I row *on* the Ohio, not *in* it."

"Do you wear a life jacket?"

"I have one in the boat, but I don't wear it. It gets in the way. Plus, I'm strapped in at the chest, and both hands are secured to the oars. What good is a life vest going to be if I flip over?" I say lightheartedly.

"But what happens if the boat flips?"

"I'll die happy."

And it's true.

To calm some of your doubts, I use pontoons to stabilize the boat, and a volunteer is out with me on a nearby boat when I'm in the single.

Along the way, I've tried a number of sports and activities.

Some would call these adventures risky, especially since I already have an injury. But what's the point of life if I'm not pushing the limits of my comfort zone?

In John 10:10 (NIV) Jesus says, "I have come that they may have life, and have it to the full." If we live in fear of the "what ifs," we will never *live* life.

~

Rugby probably is not the first sport that comes to mind when you think of me playing a sport. Quad rugby, or wheelchair rugby, is a contact sport for athletes with dysfunction in all four limbs. Most players are quadriplegics from spinal cord injuries, but there are also players with cerebral palsy, quadruple amputees, as well as other disabilities. Even though it's a co-ed sport, it's mostly guys on the court.

I had tried playing rugby once or twice but was intimidated by the roughness and physicality of the sport and by the guys' coarse talk and bluntness. It didn't help that after one of the first practices, I woke up the next morning with a swollen and bruised hand from some unknown injury. (I can't feel my hands, so no, it didn't hurt.) I decided to stick with tennis and rowing.

Then Jill Farmer, a recreational therapist, started a team supported by Frazier Rehab Institute. I decided to give it another try. In the fall of 2008, Jill and I would get up early and drive three hours to Nashville for a four-hour practice. It made for a long Saturday and a short weekend. But the sport was another challenge for me to attempt to conquer. And I discovered the guys weren't so scary after all.

All of the players used chairs constructed to withstand direct hits. Many describe rugby chairs as looking like something out of a doomsday movie. With gloves on my hands, I put on layers of tape, sticky side facing out, to provide a tacky surface with which to push the rims and help me catch and pass the ball. A chest strap and straps around each leg at my knee held me tightly in the chair, even on a hard impact.

Wheelchair rugby is part hockey, part soccer, and part football. It is played with a volleyball on a basketball court. Players are classified based on their ability on a scale from 0.5 (lowest function) to 3.5 (highest function). I'm classed as a 1.0. A total of 8 points per team between four players are allowed on the court at a time. The game is fast-paced, as a point is scored each time a player carries the ball across the goal line—with at least two of the four wheels crossing that line.

My main role on the court was defensive: to "pick" other players. Simply put, a picker's job is to be annoying to the other team's players. Using the front of my specially designed chair, I wedged the pick into an opponent's chair to prevent him or her from moving. Only in worst-case scenarios would I handle the ball. Even then, I didn't like or want the pressure of having the ball.

Rugby practice was always a good workout with pushing and tossing drills and splitting into teams to scrimmage. Playing in tournaments was challenging, but I enjoyed competing as a team (except when your teammates show up for a game hungover after a night of partying).

During a tournament, the gym is engulfed by the sounds of chairs colliding, metal upon metal. Tires or tubes blow upon impact making a loud booming sound. The referees' whistles signal the beginning or end of a play, a foul, a timeout, or turnovers for the ball not crossing the court in twelve seconds. Buzzers indicate the end of an eight-minute quarter. On the sidelines, the volunteer support staff helped repair blown tubes, hand out water during timeouts, or turn players and their chairs upright when someone inevitably flipped over. It certainly wasn't the calm surroundings of rowing or the polite clapping during a tennis tournament. But that's what made it so extraordinary.

The best part of playing rugby was the relationships. I'd not had close friendships or camaraderie with a group of guys since "the guys" in the band. On hours-long bus rides to tournaments in Alabama, Michigan, Ohio, Missouri, or Georgia, everything under the sun was discussed. And since it'd take so long to load all of us onto the bus via a lift, transfer into the seats, and stack all the chairs in the back of the bus, we'd have to do everything on the bus until we reached our destination.

"Everything" included going to the bathroom. This is done more discreetly than you'd assume. Guys throw a towel over their head to cath in privacy or empty a drainage bag into a soda bottle. But when I first announced, "Guys, sorry, but I have to pee," Kevin about fell over.

I laughed. "I have a stoma and cath through my belly. Don't get too excited. You're not going to see anything!"

On another occasion, several of us had to go to the bathroom at the same time. Let's just say I won a peeing contest.

When I was invited to speak at a church in Colorado, the first thing I did was call Kerry.

"I'm coming to Boulder in February. Is there any chance we can get together while I'm out there?" I asked.

"We've got to go skiing, Jen!"

Somehow, I knew that was coming. Kerry had been trying to get me to go downhill skiing for years.

With a deep exhale, I said, "I'll give anything a try once."

I met Kerry at the Mazatlán sports camps in Mexico where she was an able-bodied volunteer. On one infamous night at a *discoteca*, she managed to get me on the dance floor with the rest of the group. Soon after, I needed to pee. In true Mexican style, with no accessible bathroom, Kerry helped me use a Corona beer bottle to empty the catheter bag.

Kerry serves as a wonderful example to me of what truly living life looks like. She's an avid skier, horseback rider, and community volunteer. Her zest for life—as a single woman several decades ahead of me—is an example I hope to emulate.

Kerry was true to her word and set up the skiing adventure. We headed up to Keystone Ski Resort where the Breckenridge Outdoor Education Center has adaptive ski equipment and instructors.

I came prepared with warm layers of clothing after a run in with hypothermia while snow tubing a decade earlier. Breckenridge Outdoor Education Center also was well aware of the issues with temperature regulation of disabled skiers. I wore wool socks, long underwear, pants, legwarmers, and snow pants. Just on my bottom half. I wore an Under Armour long-sleeved shirt, a fleece pullover, my black North Face jacket, a bright orange puffer coat, and an additional wind- and water-resistant jacket on top. Two sleeping bags also went over my legs. The final touches included a neck gaiter, ski goggles, and a helmet. I was exhausted simply by getting dressed.

Then it was time to get in the sit-ski. There are several types of sit-skis for disabled skiers. With my higher-level injury, I used a bi-ski that had a bucket seat and two skis, instead of one, to provide additional stability. I also held an outrigger in each hand with the assistance of gloves and Velcro straps to balance and lean into turns. As a beginner, I was tethered to an able-bodied ski instructor who taught me how to control the bi-ski and took over when needed.

Having skied only once before my injury, I assumed we would start on the bunny hills. I quickly discovered there are no bunny hills in Keystone. We headed straight toward the ski lift where I learned how to get onto the lift with assistance.

The ride to the top of the snow-covered mountain was breathtaking. Tall dark fir trees covered the sides of the mountains, while the sun shone in a bright blue sky dotted with wispy white clouds.

We timed getting off the ski lift just right and glided to the beginning of the trail. My stomach dropped as I looked down a ski slope so steep that the end wasn't even visible.

Well, there's only one way down! I told myself.

With Kerry's support, my instructor, Ella, began to guide me down the slope, explaining how to lean into the turns and use the outriggers for support. Holding two straps attached to the bi-ski, Ella would release or pull as necessary to help me turn the ski in the proper direction.

"Right turn. Good. Now down the hill. Left turn. Down the hill. Good job!" Ella encouraged.

Until I skied down a mountain, I don't think I had an appreciation of how high mountains are. We arrived at the bottom intact, but the muscles in my arms, back, and neck were tired from the exercise. After a quick breather, we headed back to the lift and skied down a second time. I was feeling a bit more confident.

We ate lunch in the resort, then hit the slopes again. Although the high was only twenty degrees that day with a chilly breeze, I was able to shed one jacket before we headed back to the lift. The afternoon sky was overcast, but the morning sun and skiers had packed the snow, making the trails rough and a bit slick. Kerry skied ahead of us to record me coming down the mountain. All looked well until I leaned a little too far to my right and couldn't recover, falling onto my side. I crashed and burned. And I lived to tell about it.

Although Kerry tells me I'm a natural, skiing isn't exactly my cup of tea. The momentum I picked up going down the ski slopes was controlled only by Ella holding me back when necessary. For someone who likes to be in control, that was unnerving. In all honesty, I can say I prefer the gentle current, or even a strong current, of the Ohio River to the breakneck speed of flying down the side of a mountain. Despite the fear, a smile was glued to my face the entire time. I'm surprised it didn't freeze there.

The relaxing rhythm of rowing, the clanging of metal against metal in rugby, and the breathtaking speed of skiing down a mountain are the building blocks of a full and abundant life. But I had to be willing to say, "I'll try anything once." You never know what you might find as you stretch beyond the familiar and into the impossible.

CHAPTER TWENTY-FIVE

In the fall of 2008, I scheduled another wheelchair distribution in Afghanistan. Actually, I rescheduled the trip. For well over two years, I had been trying to return to Afghanistan, but the organization's budget proved to be an issue.

During this time, I read a verse that caught my attention: "Dear brothers and sisters, after we were separated from you for a little while (though our hearts never left you), we tried very hard to come back because of our intense longing to see you again. We wanted very much to come to you, and I, Paul, tried again and again, but Satan prevented us" (I Thess. 2:17-18 NLT). Even Paul was stopped for a short time from going to a place he wanted to be. I continued to work and wait on God's timing.

I was now the co-vice president of the Mobility Project and felt confident in my role to organize this outreach. After almost two years, I had the funding for the trip and had shipped the chairs to Afghanistan via the USAID's Denton Program, which allows organizations to use available space on US military cargo planes to transport humanitarian goods at no cost.

We were all set.

One month before the distribution, I received a call from a board member.

"I hate to be the one to tell you, but the board canceled the trip. The funds have been used for other purposes. I'm sorry, Jen."

I hung up the phone and cried, not only for the cancellation of the trip but more so by the realization I'd be leaving a ministry I loved with my entire being.

I was aware of the financial state of the organization and had voiced my concerns that the funds weren't being used as intended by donors. I decided if the wheelchair distribution in Afghanistan was canceled for any reason other than security issues, I needed to resign. Although my future was uncertain, the one thing I was sure of was that I needed to follow through on this trip and finish what I had started.

While talking with an NGO that worked in Afghanistan, I learned it had a small group of volunteers traveling to Kabul two weeks after I had planned to go. I asked if the organization and its volunteers would be willing to help me distribute the wheelchairs that had already arrived in Afghanistan. The NGO hadn't made any specific plans for its volunteers, and said yes.

I would be the only person from the Mobility Project on this trip, and the only one with experience in seating and positioning wheelchairs. I raised the funds needed to travel with the new group and looked for a travel buddy. Nooria could help me in-country, but I still needed assistance on the long flights and layovers. I didn't need to look very far. I met Leah that summer at a conference concerning Afghanistan, and she already planned to go on this trip. Plus, she was a nurse. She agreed to travel with me.

Leah and I left a day before the rest of the team, allowing us to overnight in Paris to break up my travel time. Personnel at Charles de Gaulle Airport "misplaced" my chair and told me to go to the hotel without it. Let's just say I didn't leave the airport without a few words with Air France—nor without my chair. Unfortunately, broken or misplaced wheelchairs are not uncommon when traveling by air.

We met up with the group in Dubai, and all nine of us arrived in Kabul at about ten in the morning of Sunday, October 19. Upon touching down in Kabul, the men on our team had a crash course on how to help me off the plane and bump me and my chair down the steps onto the tarmac.

The changes in the country since my last visit, more than two years ago, were immediately apparent. Security at the airport had increased, and instead of our vehicles waiting for us just outside the airport, we had to walk about a half mile to the parking lots. Once in the vans, the ride to the guesthouse, the same one where I'd stayed my first two trips, took only about twenty minutes on newly paved roads lined by saplings. This was an attempt to rebuild the "City of Trees," as Kabul had once been known. There was other new construction, as well. Wedding halls seemed to be on every corner and were lit up at night like Las Vegas. And there were gas stations. I had never seen a gas station on previous visits. I saw large homes being built, made of concrete blocks with rebar sticking out the top; the houses were reportedly funded by the heroin trade.

To avoid giving in to jet lag, we kept busy that day, organizing the shipment of wheelchairs in the afternoon and visiting Camp Eggers, the US military base in Kabul, that evening. We met the chaplain and attended the Sunday evening service.

Being awake for more than twenty-four hours was taking its toll, and my eyes were heavy. But worshipping with the men and women serving in the military in Afghanistan was an honor. After the service, we sat outside in the chilly air around a bonfire talking with them about their experience in Afghanistan.

This was my first time leading a distribution by myself. Thankfully, the group of volunteers had a heart for the disabled and caught on quickly as I explained what needed to be adjusted on each chair and oversaw the administration. I also had to make the gut-wrenching decisions about who would or would not receive a wheelchair.

On Monday we went to an internally displaced persons (IDP) camp about an hour and a half from the guesthouse. Many of the people living in the IDP camp had fled to Iran or Pakistan during the fighting with Russia or the rule of the Taliban and had returned to bombed-out buildings in Kabul. The Afghan government relocated them into an expanse of dry and dusty earth, its colorless landscape framed only by distant mountains. The organization with which I was partnering supported this community by assisting with a medical clinic, school, and a well, with the hopes the camp would one day be a self-sufficient community. When I arrived, most of the families were finally living in mud-brick dwellings rather than tents that had provided little shelter from the elements. The mosque was still made from a large faded khaki tent, rectangular in shape and bolstered in the middle by four large stakes. The community still lacked electricity.

The first day of distribution went well, considering no one

had experience in seating and positioning, and the three tool-boxes I had shipped were nowhere to be found. We rummaged around and found the bare basic tools we needed. As we worked in the unfinished medical clinic with its bare cement walls and dirt floor, groups of dirty, yet beautiful, children peeked through the glassless windows to see what we were doing. The team distributed fourteen wheelchairs that day. I especially remember Mulki, a thirty-six-year-old mother, who had been unable to walk for five years. Her husband was sixty-five; her daughter brought everything to her as she sat in a corner of the house. Later that week, Mulki showed up in her new wheelchair at a food distribution.

But not everyone left happy. One man, who was able to walk with crutches, raised his voice at me when I decided not to give him a wheelchair. Delawar Khan, who worked for the NGO and interpreted for us, de-escalated the situation. I always felt safe in the presence of this large, kind man. At my instruction, he asked the angry man to come back Friday. If we had a chair left, we would give it to him.

On our next day, we drove to Istalif to distribute chairs to two boys. In comparison to Kabul and the IDP camp, Istalif, one hour north of Kabul, looked like a lush garden with its trees and running water. I've been told that the Taliban ran everyone out of the city, destroyed the irrigation systems, and burned the city to the ground in 1998. But about thirty-five thousand people—75 percent of the population—had returned. A new power plant built by the South Koreans provided electricity to the town.

Leaving Istalif, we drove to another community to distribute four more chairs. We already had measurements for the children before our arrival, but we usually brought extra chairs in case the measurements on the applications were incorrect. On this day, three additional children showed up at the medical clinic without applications, but we were able to seat them, as well. One five-year-old girl, Neelofar, had use of only her left arm. One of the extra chairs "just happened" to be a rare one-arm drive wheelchair. The chair fit her perfectly, allowing her to push and control the direction of the chair with her good arm. Another boy with cerebral palsy had terrible contractures—shortened and tight muscles and tendons—in all four limbs. It was a difficult seating that took several hours. He arrived in a wheelbarrow but left in a wheelchair.

At the end of the week, we returned to the IDP camp to distribute a few more chairs. The man who left angry earlier in the week returned, and we had a chair for him. Walibullah's leg had been damaged twelve years earlier by bullets, and he couldn't bend his knee. We had a chair with elevating leg rests that allowed him to comfortably rest his damaged limb. Walibullah, dressed in a shalwar chemise and vest, with unkempt curly hair and a long, dark beard, smiled when his picture was taken. He expressed his gratitude and apologized for being upset earlier in the week.

As we were loading the few remaining chairs and preparing to leave, a woman arrived at the clinic carrying a young girl whose hair was shaved off. Leaning in to speak with the woman covered in a burka, I learned that Shekiba could stand, but only with assistance because of weakness in all four limbs. She was not able to speak, despite being seven years old.

There was one unboxed child's chair left in the back of the truck. After taking Shekiba's measurements, I knew that chair was going to fit her with only a few adjustments. After we finished adjusting the chair, we completed packing. I looked down the dirt road and saw Shekiba's older brothers pushing her home, their mother walking behind the boys with her blue burka blowing in the wind.

I rejoiced in how God provided the perfect chair for each and every person. I was content knowing I had followed through on this project that had been laid on my heart. Each piece of the puzzle had fallen into place. Yet I felt unsettled, knowing I had an important decision to make.

During the last few nights of our time in the city, our team stayed inside after nightfall because of security concerns. The day after our arrival, Gayle Williams, a British aid worker with Serve Afghanistan, was shot and killed as she walked to work in Kabul. The Taliban claimed responsibility. I'd heard the news of her death while we were in Kabul, but it felt surreal.

Although we always had armed guards with us at the distributions, security threats seemed unfounded most of the time because the communities and leaders welcomed us in such a hospitable manner. Again, Afghanistan proved to be a paradox.

On our way back to the US, Leah and I stopped in Paris. After a brief nap, we met up with a friend from Louisville and went sightseeing. Katherine took us to a restaurant called Angelina where we ate a delicious lunch topped off with the most decadent cup of hot chocolate I will ever taste.

We walked around the city, taking in the beautiful architecture, the flowing Seine River with its bridges, and musicians playing instruments as we traveled along the cobblestone sidewalks. Paris was strikingly dissimilar to Kabul; it enchanted me.

As the three of us walked back to the hotel, I bought bread, cheese, and a small bottle of wine for a late dinner. In the room, I opened my computer and stared at a blank computer screen.

I began writing my letter of resignation to the Mobility Project.

CHAPTER TWENTY-SIX

After I resigned from the Mobility Project in 2008, I had no clue what I was going to do for a job. I found a part-time position tutoring while I continued to look for the next step.

My roommate Emily was engaged and moving to Nevada, and she invited me to the going-away party her coworkers were throwing for her. The organization Emily worked for had more than three hundred members living overseas who integrated the physical and spiritual needs in their country of service. Some taught in schools, ran businesses to employ nationals, or met the physical needs of the community, such as in medicine or community development, while others focused on the spiritual needs by making disciples of all nations (Matthew 28:19 NIV).

Sitting at a booth in Graeter's Ice Cream, I chatted with Emily and her coworkers while eating a scoop of strawberry chunk ice cream.

"I keep telling Jenny that she should apply for the member care position at work," Emily told a coworker. She had repeatedly talked to me about the position, saying I'd be perfect for it because of my educational background in counseling.

"I don't want to do counseling," I argued. I assumed the job included clinical counseling and therapy.

"What *do* you want to do?" her coworker asked.

"I'd like to continue working overseas or support others who do."

She didn't say a word, despite my response being the exact description of the position. Member care involves supporting, encouraging, and ensuring people who work cross-culturally are emotionally, spiritually, and physically healthy, as the stressors of living overseas can take a toll on overall health.

That evening I returned home and sat in front of my computer applying for more jobs in which I had little interest. Although it was not audible, I felt God telling me, "Member care *is* supporting people who work overseas."

My preconceived notions disappeared. I knew I had to eat my words. Over the weekend, I prayed about it. On the following Monday, I called the president of the organization.

"I'm ready to hear more."

Since April 2009, I've worked in the organization's home office in Louisville. When I said yes to the job, I knew I'd need to ask for some accommodations. I was going into an office with set 9 to 5 hours. With a knot in my stomach, I requested a thirty-two-hour workweek with two days working from home. I wanted—needed—to maintain my health. I believe that was the best decision I ever made, although I admit, it took some humility.

Thankfully, the organization was willing to accommodate

me. At the end of thirty-two hours, I still have enough fuel in my tank to have a life outside of work.

However, I still wanted to prove I could do my job successfully. In my effort to keep up with everyone, during my first year, I worked an insane number of hours one week while we hosted a conference. I developed a small pressure sore and ended up in bed for two weeks. That made me realize it wasn't worth trying to prove myself to my colleagues. Finding the balance between competently doing my job and taking care of myself was—and is—a balancing act.

In this position, I use that master's degree in counseling psychology that I never wanted. Through emails and calls, I listen to and encourage my coworkers as I hear the loneliness of being half a world away from friends and family, the frustration of learning a second language, and the joy when a friend decides to entrust her life to God and truly live. I review applicants' strengths and weaknesses and help them prepare before they leave. From time to time, I send short text messages of reassurance, while other times I schedule a two-hour block of time for a video chat. I educate new workers on the stressors of cross-cultural life—including culture shock, team conflict, the importance of self-care, how to avoid burnout—and help them navigate the never-ending transitions of life overseas.

Upon moving to another country, many of my coworkers struggle with the loss of identity, loss of independence, and loss of relationships. They have to learn new ways of living and how to adapt to challenging conditions. Oddly enough, these are the same issues I've had to work through over the past few decades, just in a different capacity.

I don't travel as often as I did in the past, but I still have opportunities to visit coworkers in the Middle East, Asia, North Africa, and Europe. I spoke during English Camp for kids in Spain. I've traveled to North Africa and visited the therapy center my coworkers started for children with disabilities. I babysat six kids in South Asia so their parents could go out on a date. Whether it's talking with able-bodied coworkers about their relational struggles as we traverse the cobbled streets in Rome or Istanbul or Prague, or getting carried down three flights of steps in the New Delhi airport because of power outages, I continue to have my fair share of adventures with some of the greatest people I could ever hope to work.

Though what I do isn't as newsworthy as distributing wheelchairs, my job flows from who I am. Well, more accurately, who I've become. I'm certainly not that sixteen-year-old girl with the inability to grieve losses or whose world is so tiny that I take my wheelchair for granted. I use the skills I've acquired along the way to encourage, serve, and listen to others who live and work in a cross-cultural context.

CHAPTER TWENTY-SEVEN

It was a beautiful fall day in Indiana with temperatures in the mid-seventies and a bright blue sky as Jenny Pagni, my rowing partner, and coach Bob Hurley lifted me into our silver WinTech double rowing scull. Bob kneeled beside me and pulled the black binder tightly around my abdomen which helped keep my blood pressure up. Then I grabbed the black chest strap sitting to my left on the dock. I wrapped it around the back of the red seat and under my breasts, tugging it securely and fastening the long Velcro strap, ensuring I'd not lose my balance during the race.

"Don't forget your hat," Bob joked, handing me the white sports cap I wore in addition to the black Oakley sunglasses. "I know how upset you get if you don't have your hat."

I chuckled at the memory from several years earlier when I couldn't find my hat just before a regatta in Philadelphia. I threw a panicked fit as I dug through my bag.

I slipped the hat on my head, ensuring a good fit. The wind was gusty, and I didn't want it to blow off my head.

After I strapped each Active Hands glove around my wrist,

Bob pulled the right oar to me, and I slipped the palm of my hand over the top of the oar handle, tugging a second Velcro strap firmly around my fingers and the oar, giving me a tight, but not too tight, hold. If I pulled the strap too tight, I'd lose circulation in my hand; too loose and I wouldn't pull efficiently against the oar. We repeated the step with the left oar.

Jenny P stepped into the bow of the boat. As my able-bodied rowing partner of nine years, we had the routine down pat. This was our first head race—a 5000-meter race against the clock. Our previous races had been 1000-meter sprints. My stomach flip-flopped with anticipation of a dream years in the making. My goal was simply to finish this race, preferably in less than an hour to spare me any embarrassment.

Once Jenny P was in the boat, we double-checked the oarlocks and made sure my blades were "squared" since I couldn't feather oars, as other rowers with hand function do.

"Go have some fun," Bob called out with his dry sense of humor. While Jenny P and I held our oars steady, he grabbed my blade and pushed us away from the dock.

Although we had seen the course on paper, we'd never had the opportunity to row on this large reservoir in Indianapolis. We slowly rowed toward the start, which was about 700 meters away, and waited to be called to the start. As we sat in the boat on Eagle Creek Reservoir, other boats of eight, four, doubles, and singles also were waiting.

We heard a girl in one boat say, "Look! They have pontoons. That's not fair!"

Para-rowers who use only their arms are required by the international federation for rowing to use pontoons as a safety precaution. I doubt she noticed we were rowing "arms only." We were the only adaptive boat in the race, which attracted more than 175 entries.

"Boat 209 to the start," a man called through a megaphone.

We slowly picked up speed as we neared the buoys; once the bow of the boat passed the buoys, the race against the clock began.

Starting off with ten shorter strokes as we had practiced, we got the boat moving, then settled into a steady pace to allow my blood pressure and heart rate to regulate.

With the wind blowing twenty miles per hour, we seemed to row into the wind both going south at the beginning of the course, around the buoys, and the entire course going north. Popping the oars out of the water caused us to have to push the oars against the wind before dropping them back in the water for each stroke. Since both of us were rowing on the square, the blades acted as sails, making it feel as if our pace was two steps forward, one step back.

We rowed through the confusing course, its buoys spread few and far between. Jenny P was responsible for steering the boat and had to look behind her, careful to keep the boat steady to prevent either of us from catching an oar too deeply in the water. A partner rower must match the stroke of the disabled rower's stroke, so Jenny P couldn't slide; she, too, was rowing arms only and not feathering her oars.

As we approached a bridge, closing in on 4000 meters, we could see several boats creeping closer and closer with each stroke, so we veered to the side of the course to get out of their way. Once through the bridge, we knew we were nearing the finish line.

"Another strong ten," Jenny yelled. "One, two, three . . ." She counted each stroke which allowed us to stay in unison and pull as strongly as possible despite our weary and cramping muscles.

Again and again, we pulled strong tens until we finally

heard the horn signifying that our boat had crossed the finish line.

Breathing heavily, with my arms burning from overuse, I smiled. "We did it!"

Once our times were posted, I was satisfied: we finished in forty-nine minutes and forty-five seconds. Not a great time by any means, but it was under an hour, and we finished the race.

What is it about rowing that makes me willing to get up early on the one day of the week I can sleep in? It's feeling the water move the boat up and down, side to side. It's seeing the beauty of nature from a different perspective. It's the freedom of being out of my chair.

I've now been rowing longer than I was a gymnast. The interesting part of this statement is how I worded it: I *have been* rowing versus I *was* a gymnast. My identity is not in being a rower. I've learned that if I define myself by what I do or who I am in relation to an activity, job, or another human being, it can be stripped away. For identities are only temporary.

CHAPTER TWENTY-EIGHT

I sat in my hospital room writing an article for our church newspaper entitled "Suffering Well: Approaching Hardship with Joy and Intentionality." The irony of the situation wasn't lost on me.

Multiple tubes poked out from under my hospital gown, and my body shivered with fever and pain. Instead of dulling my senses, the pain medication intensified every touch, sound, thought, and emotion. I nicknamed Dilaudid "a laxative for the emotions." I cried more often than I've ever cried.

However, my brain worked productively. I finished the article with a sigh of satisfaction.

What have I learned during the most difficult times in life? I've learned that God is present. I've learned that we can trust Him. I've learned that although I may not understand my present sufferings, He can be glorified through them.

What I didn't know was I had six more weeks in the

hospital and two more surgeries before the most difficult months of my life would pass. I would have plenty of opportunities to practice what I preached about suffering.

For the first twenty years of my injury, my bowel program worked rather well. I had to have help, but it was manageable in the scheme of things. About 2008, I started having "accidents," a really nice way of saying my body would unexpectedly expel excrement at the most inconvenient times. I'd have to leave wherever I was—work, volunteering, sports—and get cleaned up. If I did it myself, it'd take two to three hours. I could ask for help, but from whom? My personal care attendant had other clients, willing friends had children and jobs, and I didn't want my mom to help since it hurt her back.

It was a crappy situation.

I scrolled through a support group for spinal cord injuries on Facebook. I read again and again how people thought a colostomy was the greatest decision they ever made. But I didn't want a colostomy. I'm allergic to adhesives (which are an integral part of a colostomy), I was worried that a colostomy bag might not stay on while playing sports, and—let me be honest—vanity. My body image had improved, but I didn't want a bag of waste attached to my belly.

But I couldn't continue living with the constant worry: fear of leaving the house, of eating, of the skin breakdown and UTIs that resulted from incontinence.

I was at the end of my rope.

As I read through the posts, one woman mentioned she had a continent ostomy—a stoma with an internal pouch made of small bowel tissue that she emptied several times a day with a large catheter. It sounded very similar to my bladder surgery. With many questions, I did what I do best: I started researching the procedure and reached out to the contact person in Florida. The response I received said that in some instances the procedure may be considered for someone with a spinal cord injury, but a colostomy was recommended. Since I had no diseased tissue, the procedure would be removing healthy tissue. It boiled down to medical ethics.

No, I don't have diseased tissue, but what exactly is functioning right now?

I spoke with the surgeon who said he would review my medical records. I shared the information about the Barnett Continent Intestinal Reservoir (BCIR) with my urologist, rehab doctor, primary care, and two gastrointestinal doctors. Four out of the five said it sounded like a great option for my quality of life.

After much prayer and receiving insurance approval, I had the surgery in March 2018. I was willing to do anything to get out of the hell I'd been living through for nine years.

I never understood trauma.

Trauma occurs when a person experiences intense fear, helplessness, or horror. When my surgery and three-week hospital stay didn't go as expected, I began to understand what many people experience after their injuries or during extended hospital stays.

I felt intense fear when I realized my low urine output, plummeting blood pressure, and high fever were symptoms of sepsis. The staff's immediate response made it clear that my situation could be critical. I felt helpless as my body craved nourishment, but I couldn't eat or drink for ten days after each surgery. With horror, I saw fecal matter oozing from my incision and realized I would require another surgery—and ten more days without food. By the third surgery, I devoured episodes on the Food Network to satisfy my unfulfilled cravings.

For weeks on end, my body screamed, "Something is wrong!" Due to autonomic dysreflexia, I sweated profusely, my heart beat rapidly, my blood pressure fluctuated from severely low to headache-inducing high. I felt sweat trickle down my neck for the first time in decades. My muscles ached from the bone-wracking chills caused by a fever. I experienced infections, pneumonia, and repeated fistulas—tunneling wounds filled with stool. In the end, I spent sixteen weeks in the hospital and had four major surgeries.

My body and soul were traumatized.

Throughout this time, I made it a habit to get out my phone and listen to a song by the Northern Irish band Rend Collective entitled "Counting Every Blessing." The song reminded me of all the incredible blessings I was experiencing in the midst of the pain, frustration, and suffering.

My nurses were angels on earth. A nursing assistant prayed for me while I sobbed in Dilaudid-induced despair when I realized I wasn't going to have the opportunity to say goodbye to a friend in hospice. At the onset of sepsis, my nurse stayed long past her twelve-hour shift to care for me and ensure I was stable before she left. Finally, my mom was at the hospital every day to lend a helping hand, as she always has been.

Counting every blessing.

A friend I'd met in Afghanistan had a severe stroke, and she was in town at an intensive aphasia therapy program to prepare her to defend her dissertation. We were able to catch up in person and even video-chatted with Nooria during our visit. What a sweet reunion. My physical therapist cheered me up when she brought a tennis racket and allowed me to hit a few balls as part of my therapy.

Counting every blessing.

Yes, I could have wallowed in the depths of the "whys?" Instead, the song reminded me to choose to see the blessings all around me. I didn't always succeed. Sulking is much easier than trying to find the good, but choosing to see the blessings breathed hope back into my weary body and soul.

Choosing to see the positive didn't—doesn't—negate the suffering, but it allowed me to see that God was still present in the midst of it.

After four months, I was released from the hospital. I went through one week of rehab since I was so physically weak I could barely transfer or dress. My weight had dropped into the double digits, and I developed a pressure sore as a result of my emaciated body.

I am independent in my bowel program at last, and I no longer live in fear of accidents related to my bowel program. But that independence came at a cost.

However, good things are often costly. For decades I couldn't relate to others when they spoke about trauma. I now understand when a situation inexplicably brings tears, fear, or panic. Recently, my doctor told me the battery on my baclofen pump had only one year left and I will need another surgery within the next twelve months. I've had this surgery five times and never thought twice about it prior to 2018. This time, it brought me to tears. All I could envision were surgery-gone-wrong and what-if scenarios.

In Second Corinthians 1:3-4 (NLT), Paul writes, "God is

our merciful Father and the source of all comfort. He comforts us in all our troubles so that we can comfort others." I never understood trauma. Now, I do. I can comfort others as I have been comforted.

Counting every blessing.

CHAPTER TWENTY-NINE

I settled into bed, pulled up the blankets, and read Sydney's text message again:

> The one-year anniversary of my injury is tomorrow . . . Do you have anything you do to get you through the day?

I whispered a short prayer for wisdom before I started typing.

> I certainly have had my share of anniversaries. The first couple of years are the hardest. The good news is that it gets easier. Here are a few things I've learned:
>
> 1. Grieve your losses. Allow yourself to acknowledge the fact that you have lost a lot. During the first several

years, I would go back and look at my journals or pictures from the days/weeks leading up to my injury. The memories are bittersweet.

2. Celebrate. I don't mean celebrate your injury. It sounds like your family has been really supportive. Celebrate *them*. Do something special. Celebrate your friends who are with you and supporting you. I am where I am today only because of the people who have supported me.

3. Count your blessings. I don't want this to sound overly simplistic or spiritual. But look back over the past year and see how God has provided the people He's placed in your life and the new experiences you've had. Yes, we need to grieve our losses, but we can learn so much through the trials. Searching for the positives, even if it's little things, will remind you that God is still with you in the midst of tragedy.

I don't know if my advice was helpful to Sydney, but writing out those three points summarized the past thirty years of my life. Grieve. Celebrate. Count your blessings.

∼

I'm often asked if I would change what happened if I could. The simple answer is no. No, I wouldn't exchange what I've gained for what was lost. But I wouldn't mind an easier life. A life with functioning hands. A life with no worries about bladder or bowel function, skin breakdown, or UTIs. No suffocating financial burdens from health-related expenses. A life where I could take a long, hot shower—alone. Or reach the groceries on the top shelf at the supermarket. Or be able to get into the homes of my friends and family. Although my chair has given me the freedom to do many things, it still puts a physical barrier between me and the world.

But an easier life doesn't mean a better life. An easier life leaves little need for dependence on God. Less need to develop humility in asking for help. Less excitement and awe when God does the inconceivable with the little I have to offer.

Because of my injury, I've learned to grieve my losses and express my frustration. It's okay if I need a good cry on a hard day. Tears don't mean I'm not strong or don't have enough faith. Rather, it shows I'm human, not a fictional superhero with endless strength and a heart of stone.

I've learned to say "yes" even when it scares the heck out of me. I never would have ridden a rollercoaster, traveled the world, or participated in adaptive sports had I not been willing to leave the comfortable and cross into the unknown and unpredictable. My life is better for it. My world is bigger.

I've seen how one person can create a ripple effect that spills over into the lives of people they may never meet. When I serve as a peer mentor at Frazier Rehab for people with new spinal cord injuries, I often visit women with my makeup bag in tow. I want to pass along the hope Lois first gave me with that tube of mascara. I invite people to my house and show them how it's possible to live independently, just as Leslie did for me at the

Ms. Wheelchair America pageant. When I think someone is ready, I encourage them to try a sport, transfer without assistance, or drive. I hope to give them the gentle push Michael gave me that night at the tennis tournament in Arizona. I want to pass along to others the opportunity to experience endless possibilities.

I've discovered how to trust. I can trust that God is working through my life, even if I don't understand the whys and hows or when I struggle to believe His promises. I trusted Dr. Shaw's ability to improve my hand function through tendon transfers. I often have to trust people, sometimes strangers, with my personal care, to carry or lift me when things aren't accessible, or to provide financially for my ministry. When I lack faith in my physical or financial circumstances, I remember Jesus's words in Matthew 6:25 (NIV): "Therefore I tell you, do not worry about your life, what you will eat or drink; or about your body, what you will wear. Is not life more than food, and the body more than clothes?" Do not worry. I need to keep working on that one.

I've learned to accept myself and my body. I try to find my identity not in something I do, but in who I am. I don't want to judge myself based on the number of "likes" on a social media post or the affirmation I receive from others. Identity and self-acceptance will be an area of growth till my dying day.

I've learned not to say, "That's impossible." Let me clarify that statement: I believe it's physiologically impossible for me to walk again on this earth. But I won't allow that to limit what is possible. My wheelchair will not determine what I am capable of doing; it probably makes me more willing to defy others' expectations. At one time, I thought it was impossible to get dressed on my own and do much of my personal care. I told people for years that I would *never* write a book. Well, you can see how that turned out. Let's challenge one another to take *impossible* and *never* out of our vocabularies.

I've experienced that life doesn't begin when a cure for paralysis is found. Or when I get a job that pays more. Or once I get married. I've learned to keep on rolling no matter my circumstances.

A life *lived* has taken me places I never dared to imagine.

THE END

GLOSSARY OF TERMS FOR SPINAL CORD INJURIES

I n the world of spinal cord injuries, we have a vocabulary with which most able-bodied people are unfamiliar. Included below is a brief guide if you are new to the club—or to prepare you for your next conversation with someone with a spinal cord injury.

Able-bodied (AB) *noun or adjective; plural* ABs – a person without a physical disability. Examples: "Hey, I need an AB over here to help get something off the top shelf." or "The able-bodied population doesn't understand life with a disability." *Alternate form:* TAB, abbreviation for temporarily able-bodied. Not to be confused with "normal."

Accessible *adjective* – a state in which a wheelchair or a person with a physical impairment can easily and independently maneuver. Example: accessible parking, accessible bathroom stall. Inappropriate use of accessible:

"Yes, our restaurant is accessible. We have only one step." The word accessible replaces the outdated term handicap.

Autonomic dysreflexia (AD) *noun;* **dysreflexic** *adjective –* the body's response to a painful or uncomfortable stimulus, typically in persons with a T6 or higher spinal cord injury; increased heart rate and blood pressure, headache, goose bumps, sweating, and blurred vision may be symptoms. AD can cause blood pressure to increase to dangerous levels and can cause a stroke, even death, if not treated. Many medical professionals are unfamiliar with AD. Example (of adjective): "I'm dysreflexic because my bladder is full. I've got to pee!"

Bowel program *noun –* the method in which a person empties his or her bowels; often a suppository and/or digital stimulation (see definition below) is required to evacuate the bowels. "I hate Monday, Wednesday, and Friday mornings. I have to get up at six to do my bowel program. It takes about an hour and fifteen minutes."

Cath *verb –* abbreviation for catheterize; the use of a catheter to empty one's bladder. Example: "I cath about six times a day."

Catheter *noun –* a tube made of silicon, PVC, red rubber, or latex that is inserted into the urethra or stoma to empty the bladder of urine; a catheter can be used several times a day (intermittently) or left in for several weeks (Foley catheter); closed-system, straight tip, coude tip, hydrophilic, and external male catheters (condom catheters) are just a few of the types of catheters available.

Chuck *noun* – a disposable pad with absorbent material and plastic underside that protects bedding or other surfaces from urine or stool.

Complete/incomplete injury *noun* – a complete injury refers to no feeling or function below the level of injury; a person with an incomplete injury has some feeling or function below the level of injury. A complete injury does not mean the spinal cord has been physically severed; very few people actually sever their spinal cords. The ASIA Impairment Scale provides a more clearly defined description of complete and incomplete.

Dig stim *noun* – abbreviation for digital stimulation; the use of a dil stick (see definition) or a gloved, lubricated finger in a circular motion inside the rectum that causes the anal sphincter and bowel muscles to relax and, in turn, allows stool to leave the body. (TMI, I know.)

Dil stick *noun* – an adaptive device that assists with digital stimulation for quadriplegics.

Disabled *adjective* – related to or having a disability; is *not* synonymous with handicapped (see below).

Electric chair *noun* – a device first used in the 1880s to execute inmates; not to be confused with a power chair, a means of mobility for some people with disabilities.

Gimp *noun* – a term of endearment for a fellow wheelchair user or person with a disability; be cautious in using this term if you are an AB.

Gimpy *adjective* – describing one's disabled-ness or gimpy-ness.

Handicap *noun*, **handicapped** *adjective* – can be an offensive term for a person with a disability; the words *disability* or *disabled* is preferred. A few theories exist on the word's origin: 1) Handicap is derived from an old English game "hand in cap," a game in which two people traded items and had an equal chance of winning. 2) It was used in the late eighteenth century in horse racing, with the better horse having to carry more weight (a handicap) to even the odds. The term came to mean a disadvantage that makes success unusually difficult.[1]

Hand controls *noun* – mechanical devices on a vehicle that allow a person with a disability to control the brake and gas with their upper extremities; hand controls may be a simple push/pull system or a complicated computerized system where a joystick controls the steering, brake, and gas.

Invols (abbreviation for involuntary) or **accidents** *noun, plural* – when the bladder or bowel revolts and expels its contents unexpectedly. Expletives or despair may follow this crappy situation in which one finds himself or herself.

Manual chair *noun* – a wheeled mobility device propelled by the user.

Paraplegic *noun*, **para** *abbreviation* – a person with impairment in the trunk and lower extremities; typically refers to persons with thoracic- or lumbar-level spinal cord injuries. Honest (albeit somewhat faulty) thoughts from a quadriplegic: "Paras have it made. They can use their hands."

Person-first terminology – wording used that focuses on the person, not the disability. Example: People with disabilities vs. disabled people.

Power wheelchair, power chair *noun* – a wheeled mobility device powered by batteries; costs more than many automobiles.

Pressure relief/weight shift *noun* – relieving the pressure and weight off one's rear end or other body part allowing blood flow in order to maintain healthy tissue and to prevent pressure sores; ideally, pressure relief is done every fifteen to thirty minutes by lifting one's body, leaning side to side or forward, or tilting backward in a power chair.

Pressure sore, skin breakdown *noun* – a wound that develops when blood flow is reduced or eliminated and causes injury or death to the surrounding tissue; formerly referred to as a bed sore. Medical term: decubitus ulcer.

Quad belly/para belly/quad pod *noun* – the protrusion of the abdomen and intestines because of the lack of abdominal muscles in quads and paras. "Miss Jenny, are you pregnant?" "No, that's just my quad belly."

Quadriplegic *noun,* **quad** *abbreviation* – a person with impairment in all four limbs; does not mean complete loss of arm function; quadriplegics may maintain use of the arms, but not the full use of their hands or fingers. The term *tetraplegic* is becoming more common in the medical field; the root word *plegia* is Greek meaning "paralysis"; *quadra* is Latin, while *tetra* is Greek, both meaning "four."

Quadly *adjective* – appearing or behaving like a quadriplegic. "My quadly hands can't pick up anything today."

SCI/D *noun* – abbreviation for spinal cord injury/disorder; SCIs are most often caused by a traumatic event or injury; but strokes, tumors, and other diseases also can damage the spinal cord.

Sliding board/transfer board *noun* – a plastic or wooden board that is placed under the rear end of its user in order to provide a solid surface on which to move; used for getting in or out of bed, vehicles, showers, etc.

Spasms, spasticity *noun* – uncontrolled movement in the extremities caused by wayward messages in the nervous system; spasms may occur at and/or below the level of injury; severity varies from person to person.

Tenodesis *noun* – the use of wrist extensor and flexor muscles in quadriplegics to grip objects; wrist extension causes the thumb and fingers to pull together allowing a quad to pick up an object, while wrist flexion releases the item.

Transfer *noun, verb* – the act of lifting or moving one's body (either independently or with assistance) from one place to another. Example: "I'm going to transfer into bed now."

UTI *noun* – abbreviation for urinary tract infection; an infection in the bladder, urethra, ureters, or kidneys. UTIs were once the leading cause of death for persons with spinal cord injuries.

References

1. Douglas Baynton, "Language Matters: Handicapping an Affliction," Disability History Museum, accessed August 4, 2020, http://www. disabilitymuseum.org/dhm/edu/essay.html?id=30.
2. *Merriam-Webster Dictionary Online*, s.v. "handicap," accessed October 18, 2017, Handicap. Merriam-Webster. https://www.merriam-webster.com/ dictionary/handicap.

ACKNOWLEDGMENTS

To my family and friends, thank you for your support throughout this crazy, wonderful life I've lived. To say anything more would require pages. It is *you* I celebrate every July 11th.

Editors are now among my highest esteemed people in the writing process. Beth Jusino, thank you for teaching me how to make words on a page come to life. Passive verbs be darned. Ellen Wolkensperg, thank you for graciously line editing each draft. Kathy Burge, thank you for the finishing touches in the editorial process.

I can't leave out Ruth Schenk. You encouraged me—even before I began writing. And Lisa Dickman, your feedback during our long walks not only improved my writing but lifted my spirits during a difficult year. Now it's your turn to write.

Ben Wolf, thank you for answering my one thousand and one questions regarding publishing.

Last but not least, Chip MacGregor, thank you for believing in my writing. If not for you, my story would still be on the hard drive of my computer. Thank you for your time and knowledge. You deserve more than a box of bourbon truffles.

About Jenny Smith

When Jenny was sixteen years old, she sustained a C6-7 spinal cord injury that left her paralyzed from the chest down. After completing her master's degree in counseling psychology, she distributed wheelchairs for eight years in developing countries.

Since 2009 she has worked with an international non-profit organization to ensure its workers stay healthy emotionally, physically, and spiritually while living cross-culturally.

Jenny is a dynamic speaker and shares her motivational and educational message with students, medical professionals, associations, and faith-based groups as well as through writing on her website. She mentors patients with newly acquired spinal cord injuries and is a member of the Kentucky Community Crisis Response Team.

A self-proclaimed nerd, Jenny enjoys researching family history, reading a variety of genres of books, and studying languages. She loves interacting with peoples from different cultures and cherishes time with her niece and nephew.

Rowing on the Ohio River and playing wheelchair rugby are just a few of the ways she stays physically active.

Follow Jenny on her website or on social media:
www.JennySmithRollsOn.com

Sign up for her mailing list: https://bit.ly/3vcZ6mJ

instagram.com/jenny.smith.rolls.on
facebook.com/JennySmithRollsOn
youtube.com/JennySmithRollsOn

Made in the USA
Monee, IL
15 July 2021

73690929R00142